MISSION-SHAPED
GRACE

Missional Practices for Missional Disciples

JOHN MᶜGINLEY

RIVER
PUBLISHING

River Publishing & Media Ltd
Bradbourne Stables
East Malling
Kent ME19 6DZ
United Kingdom

info@river-publishing.co.uk

Illustrations by Nathan Obokoh.
Nathan Obokoh Artistic
nathanobokoh.com

Published in partnership with New Wine Trust

www.new-wine.org

ISBN 978-1-908393-66-1
Cover design by www.spiffingcovers.com
Printed in the United Kingdom

Contents

Acknowledgements

Grateful thanks...

...to the staff and congregation of Holy Trinity Church who are my family on mission – you constantly inspire me to be better and to keep going on this incredible journey.

...to my friends in the New Wine family who have kept me alive in God and opened up to me the wonders of the Kingdom.

...to Pete, Sarah, Lorraine and Hilary for your help in preparing the content of this book and to Tim Pettingale at River Publishing for your support and patience with me.

...to Bridget, whose love and support have been my strength ever since we made our promises.

What Others Are Saying...

"A wonderful guide to what it truly means to be a disciple. Immensely practical, and equally inspiring, this book will help you to powerfully share the Gospel and make disciples. Buy it today and put the words on its pages into action."
Gavin Calver
Director of Mission / England, Evangelical Alliance

"There is a renewed passion in the Church today for mission, but it often seems that we have forgotten how to go about it. Some approaches to mission feel forced and out of touch with the modern world; with others it is hard to imagine Jesus and the disciples engaging in the same practices. Thoroughly biblical and proven in the life of his own church, John's approach is neither, offering instead encouragement and great wisdom for leaders who want to equip their congregations for today's mission context. Highly recommended!"
Paul Harcourt
National Leader of New Wine England

"There is no greater commission, no higher calling given to us than to make disciples of nations and peoples. John skilfully unpacks how to do this from a foundation and motivation of the great love and grace we have all received. Each of us are ambassadors of reconciliation to the lost, bringing them to their heavenly Father. *Mission-Shaped Grace* will help you understand how to do this in a very practical and powerful way."
Dr Jonathan Oloyede
National Day of Prayer UK

"Making disciples matters. It really does. It's an eternal investment of our time and energy. In this inspiring book – rooted in passion and experience – John brings a refreshing perspective and practical application to help us all realise that we can do this! We must do this! And this book will show us how."
Matt Summerfield
President, Urban Saints & Senior Pastor, Hitchin Christian Centre

"John's passion for mission, and experience in discipleship and leadership, overflow on to the pages of *Mission-Shaped Grace*, in words have been lived out before the ink ever went near the page. If you've ever wondered not just the 'if', but also the 'how' of mission, then this book, which is packed full of stories, is for you."
Revd Barry Hill
Mission Enabler, Diocese of Leicester

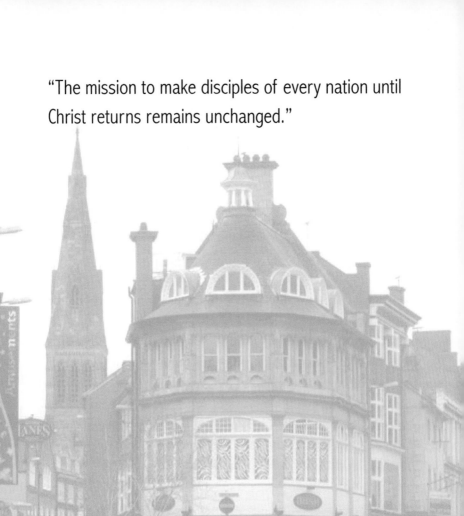

"The mission to make disciples of every nation until Christ returns remains unchanged."

1
Introduction

As I write this, I am sitting looking over the wonderful city of Leicester in a coffee shop with a bird's-eye view of the city. There are people chatting and chilling and shopping in the midst of the 300,000 people with whom we share this city. And I sit here with a responsibility towards them – for I know the greatest secret of human life – that God loves them, and in Jesus he has acted decisively to open up the way back home to him. So here is my dilemma: *how do I let them know this amazing news in a way that can help them come back into relationship with their heavenly Father?* I could stand on my chair and preach (and I'm pretty good at that!) and yet that would simply annoy them as I spoiled the relaxation of this place. And, because I have no relationship with them, it would probably confirm their prejudices against Christians as those who shout at people and sit in judgement over them. But I cannot simply rest easy with excuses, because in the Good News of Jesus there is a love and a compulsion that requires that I share it (2 Corinthians 5:14). And so I turn my thoughts to those with whom I share my life on a regular basis who don't know Jesus. *How can God use me to show them his existence and love?*

The mission to make disciples of every nation until Christ

returns remains unchanged. If the work of mission is like building a bridge between God and lost people, then the Church's bridge has become disconnected from the lives of people around us. We remain connected to God on one end, but the society around us has shifted, so that the way we have learned to do mission in the past no longer overcomes the barriers it used to. The reality of our failure to do this effectively in the West is stark. I recently heard of a study that suggested 86% of churches in the USA and Europe will not reproduce themselves by planting another church community – and a similar percentage of individual Christians will never lead someone to put their faith in Jesus.

Mission-Shaped Grace is an attempt to capture what I believe God has been teaching us about mission in our culture and how we can reach those friends, colleagues and family members with the Good News of Jesus Christ. It presents ways in which we can partner with the Holy Spirit in connecting his presence with others. Within this book you will find five missional practices for 21st century missional disciples:

Generosity

Receiving and Releasing

Asking Questions and Telling Stories

Calling

Eating Together

1. **G**enerosity: living generously and taking opportunities to bless others

2. **R**eceiving and Releasing God's Presence: being filled with the Holy Spirit and learning to recognise and respond to the presence of God in any situation

3. **A**sking Questions and Telling Stories: the art of loving, God-filled conversation

4. **C**alling: understanding your unique contribution to God's mission

5. **E**ating together: sharing your life with others.

As you can see, they are all very simple, but at the same time they are deeply profound when offered up to God and to others in the power of the Spirit and with love. They are ways that reflect the relational character of God and how he has created us to live. Each Christian is called and equipped by the Holy Spirit to reveal God to the world around them and, therefore, the pattern of this mission has to be accessible to all of us. The Christian faith was never meant to be clever or complicated (1 Corinthians 1:26-27). As Mother Theresa said, "Don't try to do great things for God. Do small things with great love." To be honest, I want to do great things for God and I hope I will, but Jesus teaches us that the kingdom of God often grows from small to large. So let's start small and see what our great God can do with our humble offerings. Starting small also takes away our excuses, because each one of these practices is possible for every Christian – not just the superstars with airplane testimonies.

The first letters of each of these phrases spell GRACE because the aim of these practices is to live lives filled with God's grace. Most Christians I know long for the people who they love to come to know Jesus, but the silent cry of our heart is "Yes, but how?!" I am convinced that following these practices will enable each one of us to see the grace of God flow through us and touch others' lives. And the reason that I am convinced is because I and others I know have used them and seen God draw people to himself as we did.

It was Dietrich Bonhoeffer who first coined the term "cheap grace". He was reflecting that so many Christians receive God's grace without repenting or allowing Jesus Christ to transform their lives. *Mission-Shaped Grace* comes from the understanding that as we receive the grace of God it has within it a call to mission and to share it with others that should shape our lives. In its nature grace is "mission-shaped" because it comes from the God of mission, and we have only received it because of his relentless pursuit of his lost creation. But the Church is no longer shaped by its missionary calling and so the grace of God becomes a stagnant pool instead of an ever-flowing stream. We must learn again how mission must be the framework of our discipleship so that God's grace can reach others through us.

Originally, the basic content of this book was developed as a resource for the members of Holy Trinity Church, Leicester, the Christian community that I have the privilege of leading as Vicar. They are the ordinary heroes of this story who have been willing to have a go and whose testimonies I tell in this book. They show that we can grow in confidence in mission and others can come to salvation in Jesus Christ through us. And it is because of their encouragement that I have developed these principles into a book which I hope will equip you in the mission you have been called to.

Imagine if each week you lived in such a way that you

intentionally blessed someone, or in the midst of your workplace or family you prayed for someone and managed to connect the Gospel story with their lives through relevant and easy conversation, or that you shared a meal with someone in which God's peace and presence was there in the friendship you gave and received. That is what I think it looks like for the kingdom to come in the midst of 21st Century Western culture. And I want to say right at the beginning that I believe we can all do this and so you *can* do it.

There is a story of the siege of Samaria during Elisha's ministry in 2 Kings 7 that reflects the challenges facing the Church today. Four men suffering from leprosy discovered that the Aramean army, who had besieged the city, had been scattered by God. The city was now free and safe, but its inhabitants were unaware of this and so the men had a dilemma. Due to their leprosy, they were not welcome in the city, but they were the only ones who knew about this freedom. They have to choose between selfishly enjoying the food and plunder, left behind by the retreating army, or risking approaching the city. They said to each other, *"What we're doing is not right. This is a day of good news and we are keeping it to ourselves."* (2 Kings 7:9).

As Christians today we face a similar dilemma. Our culture has rejected the Christian faith and we can feel the temptation to hide away and enjoy the blessings of God's kingdom by ourselves. But we are the only ones who know the Good News of the freedom Jesus has won for everyone. We cannot keep this good news to ourselves. This is a day of good news – let's share it.

Structure

This book is arranged in two sections.

Section 1 establishes something of the key principles of missional discipleship. It is in this section that we will examine some of the foundations for this approach and seek to remove some of the inherited assumptions and obstacles that often undermine us living as missional disciples of Jesus Christ. At the end of each of these foundational chapters you are encouraged to "press pause" and reflect on what work God wants to do within you in preparation for mission.

Section 2 is where we get stuck into these five missional practices. We will explore each practice from three angles:

1. Principle

God has revealed himself to us and this revelation is recorded in Scripture. The only basis on which we can have confidence in how he is calling us to live is if it "lines up" with what we read in the Bible. These practices take us back to the way Jesus lived and what we see happening in the early Church. Biblical principles will inform all that is written here, but we are called to live them out, not just learn and agree with them. The "doing" of Scripture is what *Mission-Shaped Grace* is all about.

2. Presence

These practices are good in and of themselves in helping us to live in community with others and with God. But unless we are doing them with God's love and presence in us they will simply become another thing to add to our endless "to do" lists – an additional pressure on us to work harder as a Christian.

The only way in which doing such simple things can ever make a difference in God's kingdom is if God is present to use them. Jesus said in John 5:17, *"My Father is always at his work to this very day, and I too am working."* So mission becomes less about what we are doing and more about finding out what God is doing and joining in. It is releasing to live out these simple practices in the midst of our lives in the knowledge that God's Spirit is leading us and empowering us and taking our humble offering and using it to fulfil the Father's will.

Calling these practices *Mission-Shaped Grace* is deliberate as it is only God's grace that we have to offer others. Sometimes we misunderstand what grace is. We can reduce it to merely the attitude which led God to come to this world in Jesus and die for us. Undoubtedly that was the grace of God, but grace is so much more than just an attitude or God's predisposition towards us. Out of his great love God gave *himself*. He didn't just send a message of good news, he chose to send his very self into this world. So grace is the gift of God's presence, which contains all of his favour, power, goodness and blessing for us.

When Paul heard God say to him in his struggles, *"My grace is sufficient for you"* (2 Corinthians 12:9) God wasn't just saying, "It's OK, Paul I'm on your side." He was saying, "I am with you and my presence will strengthen you." So God's grace can be understood as God's empowering presence. And as we intentionally use these missional practices we are seeking God's empowering presence for ourselves, with a desire that his presence will flow through us and touch others. We give ourselves to God and to others and we become the bridge across which God's grace can flow.

When the Greek philosopher Aristides wrote to the Roman Emperor Hadrian early in the second century AD to give his report of the early Church in Athens, he described Christians in this way: "I understood that he who moves them is God, who is hidden in them, and veiled by them. And it is manifest that that which causes motion is more powerful than that which is moved." We need the power and presence of the Holy Spirit so that those who know us can only conclude, "God is in them."

3. Practice

Throughout history Christians have found help in repeatable patterns of life that enable us to cooperate with God and create space for the Spirit to give us life.

They have called these patterns Spiritual Disciplines. A spiritual discipline is an intentionally directed action which places us in a position to receive from God the power to do what we cannot accomplish on our own. This is what these missional practices are designed to do. Here is how Richard Foster describes it in his book *Life With God*:

"The deep waters of God's life are already flowing. We simply learn the strokes that will enable us more and more to be at home in them."

And I love how *The Message* translation expresses Jesus' words in which he explains how we find rest and freedom when we learn to copy and practice his ways:

"Are you tired? Worn out? Burned out on religion? Come to me. Get away with me and you'll recover your life. I'll show you how to take a real rest. Walk with me and work with me — watch how I do it. Learn the unforced rhythms of grace. I won't lay anything heavy or ill-fitting on you. Keep company

"Practising these missional 'steps' may feel clunky to start with, but with perseverance they will become freely expressed patterns of life that the Spirit can empower."

with me and you'll learn to live freely and lightly." (Matthew 11:28-30)

Another way to look at it is through *Strictly Come Dancing!* During Week 1 the contestants are practising the dances and counting their steps. It is clunky, lacks flow and freedom, and they are stepping on toes. But by the end of the series those who are left are dancing freely, wonderfully expressing themselves. Practice and repetition has brought freedom.

Practising these missional "steps" may feel clunky to start with, but with perseverance they will become freely expressed patterns of life that the Spirit can empower. If you understand nothing else from this book, understand this: *repetition is the key to becoming comfortable in the ministry and mission of the Holy Spirit*. Being a disciple doesn't just happen naturally, it comes through repeated practice.

Once we have looked at each practice from these three angles you will be encouraged to "press play" and go and do something practical as a first step to get you going. There is also a Bible passage and questions to use individually or in a small group to enable us to apply it to our lives.

The mission statement of the church I lead is: Holy Trinity Church is a community of missional disciples that will transform the city of Leicester and beyond with the Gospel of Jesus Christ.

This vision is big and beyond our ability to achieve in our own strength. And it won't be achieved by church programmes or buildings or institutional initiatives. But it can be achieved by ordinary followers of Jesus living the Spirit-empowered missional life God has called us to live and then seeing others join us in following him. *How do I know this?* Because God has done it again and again throughout the history of the

Church and is doing it today in places like China, Iran and South America. I believe God is preparing his Church in the West for a revival that will result in the salvation of millions and the turning back of countries to his ways. We need to prepare ourselves, not just by praying and waiting for revival, but by ushering it in by living as if it is here already. These practices are a step in the right direction.

And finally a story: it comes from a concert by the brilliant 19th/20th Century Polish concert pianist, Ignacy Jan Paderewski. Just before Paderewski was about to walk onto the stage for a major recital, a 9-year old boy managed to break free from his mum and made a bee-line to that shiny grand piano in front of them. Apparently the boy had been taking piano lessons for a few months, so he fearlessly made his way up onto that piano bench and began playing his version of Chopsticks.

While this was cute for a moment or two, the sophisticated audience had little patience for this kid. Suddenly, however, Paderewski makes his way onto the stage. To everyone's surprise, instead of getting mad, he simply approaches the piano, puts his arm around the boy, and starts to improvise alongside this kid's version of Chopsticks. Now they're playing a duet! And all the time that they are playing, Paderewski whispers to the boy, "Keep playing, just keep playing."

My hope and prayer is that the teaching in this book will equip you and release you to be the missional disciple of Jesus Christ that you are. And as you read it, you will hear the Father whispering to you, "Keep playing, just keep playing."

Part 1
Principles of Missional
Discipleship

Chapter 1
What's the Story?

As Christians it is vital we understand that is our job to share the Gospel – there is a "given-ness" to the story. In Jesus and his Gospel is the radical, life-altering, world-shaking assertion that the kingdom of God has arrived. The Good News that Jesus announced with his lips, demonstrated with his life, sealed on the cross, and inaugurated with his resurrection is nothing short of the reality that the reign of God is no longer just in heaven, but is here on earth and available to all people. The biblical story of the kingdom has a shape and a goal that must be observed and to which appropriate response must be made.

The amazing truth is that God has entrusted this wonderful news to you and me. When Jesus returned to heaven I imagine a conversation with the angels that went something like...

Angels: We praise you Lord for all you have done. Now what's the plan?

Jesus: The plan is to help to protect and strengthen my disciples as they spread the Good News of the Kingdom.

Angels: OK, Lord. But there must be another plan. What if they blow it or give up or get it wrong? This is too precious to trust to those guys.

Jesus: There is no other plan.

And there is no other plan. Jesus has chosen you and me to share the Good News of the kingdom. We have come into relationship with him because the first disciples didn't blow it and then those they passed it onto carried it forward. An unbroken chain of people who kept sharing the Gospel links us to the first disciples. We need to be determined that the "chain" of the Gospel that has reached us, will not end with us. Will your life be a *cul-de-sac*, a dead end, which the Gospel story entered but never continued?

But our job is not simply to repeat the story parrot fashion in the way that others have told it but, as every Church of England vicar promises at their ordination, "to proclaim it afresh in every generation." So we have some double-listening to do: to listen to the Gospel and to listen to the lives of those around us, and then to live it out in ways that show its relevance and how it is good news for them. In other words, to have open on our Ipad the Bible App and the Youtube Channel and to learn how to connect the two.

Tom Wright explains this living out of God's story with the idea of an unfinished Shakespearean play. Imagine that an unfinished Shakespeare play is discovered, whose fifth act has been lost. The first four acts provide such clear characterisation and direction of plot that people want it to be staged. Rather than write one fixed version of the final act, it is decided to give the key parts to experienced Shakespearean actors who would immerse themselves in the first four acts and, from their knowledge of Shakespeare and his time, could work out a fifth act for themselves. The fifth act would need to be consistent with all that is contained in the first four, but the actors would need to improvise to draw out the conclusions of the play.

The parallels with the story of God's kingdom are seen in 5 Acts: (1) Creation; (2) Fall; (3) Israel; (4) Jesus. The New Testament then forms the first scene in the fifth act as the Holy Spirit is poured out on the Church. He leads the actors in this scene to fulfil our role until the final act is complete and Jesus returns.

So as God's people today we need to live under the authority of the biblical story, we have to immerse ourselves in the story and then we improvise and live it out as we play our part in God's amazing story of salvation. This helps us to understand why it is so important that we know the story! It is only as we know and understand God's word that we can faithfully live it out within our generation.

The other reason that it is important to know the Gospel story is because it is powerful. The Gospel really is the power of God to save everyone who believes (Romans 1:16), and the Bible really is the word of God which he promises will not return to him without producing fruit (Isaiah 55:11). One of the challenges we have to address in the Church in the UK is that we have lost confidence in the power of God's word to reveal God and to draw people to him. It has an innate power and authority because it has been inspired by the Holy Spirit and the Holy Spirit accompanies it as it is preached and read.

J. B. Phillips was translating the New Testament from Greek to modern English 40 years ago and said afterwards, "[I] felt rather like an electrician rewiring an ancient house without being able to turn the mains off." Too often we have tried to win people for Christ through clever techniques and gimmicks instead of presenting the truth of God's word and letting it do its work. A number of the missional practices are designed to enable us to share the Gospel and Bible stories with people in a way that allows God to speak to them. Charles Spurgeon once wrote about having confidence in the Bible in this way:

"Open the door and let the lion out; he will take care of himself."

Without confidence in the goodness and power of the Gospel and God's word we will be tempted to water it down. We might try and remove the "stumbling blocks" which can offend people, such as sin, judgement, repentance and hell. Yet these are integral to the Gospel because they are the realities that people must face up to if they are to be saved. When people are heading towards a cliff edge, the most loving action is not to pretend there isn't a cliff. The most loving action is to warn them and give them the opportunity to turn around. We might try and compensate for what we see as the irrelevance of the Gospel by creatively dressing it up in more relevant clothes, reframing it within current issues.

Once we have confidence in its message, we have to avoid the opposite temptation of becoming lazy and not taking time to understand how to communicate the Gospel relevantly. Too often this has reduced the Gospel to a statement on a sandwich board or T-shirt, or to single verse soundbites. We simply proclaim it without care or creativity and then bemoan people's lack of response to it. And we have reduced what salvation looks like to getting people to "pray the prayer", as if our job is just to ensure that when a person goes through the divine supermarket checkout they have the correct barcode on them that says "prayed the prayer" and they are processed in to heaven.

This reductionist approach will not do. The full story of Scripture is of encountering the life-transforming grace of

God which turns our lives around and opens us up to the joys of living within this creation in relationship with our loving Father. That has to affect everything because, as Jesus said, the whole of the mission of God is heading towards a time when Jesus will reign and bring about the *"renewal of all things"* (Matthew 19:28).

But what does it look like to proclaim this story relevantly in our society today? These missional tools are designed to help us do this job. They are confident without being crass and creative without compromising. They are rooted in the principles and practices from Scripture and at the same time reflect the cultural attitudes of our friends which we have to work with. They will enable us to build healthy friendships within which God can enter into and we can use them to walk alongside others on the journey of discipleship.

A Love Story

Ultimately, the Christian faith is a love story and this has to affect how we share God's good news and how we help people to follow him – doing it in relationship with God and in loving relationship with those we are reaching out to, rather than any narrow programme. Please don't misunderstand me, I am not opposed to evangelistic events and street evangelism because I love any way that we can begin to connect people to God. But I am interested in every Christian living a life that builds healthy loving relationships and that carries the presence of God into their families, friendships and workplaces.

The call to mission is a call to love, as Paul writes, *"without love it is worth nothing"* (1 Corinthians 13). Our mission is a response to his love and an incarnation of his love in us. It is important that before we look at being active in mission we ground it in the love of God. As St Augustine stated,

"If the entire Bible could be encapsulated in a single sentence then it would cry out like the resounding waves of the sea, 'The Father loves you.'"

His Kingdom is a kingdom of love and so the life of discipleship must also be a life of love. We are already stressed and frantic enough and so we don't need more things added to our to-do lists or more guilt-induced pressure. Without love the tools taught in section 2 of this book will, at best, become a tick-list of Christian behaviours and at worst be like sales techniques. But with love they become the channels that love can flow through to touch a broken world.

Equally, we must not reduce love to sentimental emotionalism in which no hard work is allowed. It is too easy an excuse for us to trot out that we step back from intentionally witnessing about God's love to our friends because we fear being manipulative. Love is always intentional and determined, as well as spontaneous and emotional. The love of a parent for their child causes them to intentionally try to become better parents. They read baby care and parenting books, search internet sites for advice, and then to apply that shared wisdom in their parenting practice. As those who love our friends and family members who don't know their Heavenly Father, the most loving thing we can ever do is to learn how to, and intentionally look for ways to share Jesus with them.

In understanding that love is the heartbeat of mission I have found the way that others have expressed the Christian life as three directions or relationships of love:

Covenant (UP) – loving and being loved by God:
Passionate Spirituality
Community (IN) – loving our Christian brothers and sisters:
Radical Community
Kingdom (OUT) – loving the last, least and lost:
Missionary Zeal

Because we use the word "love" to refer to a general approval or enjoyment of something, it can be a bit of a blunt word. I can say that I love football and fast food, as well as my wife and children. So for each of the three relationships there is an adjective that communicates the quality that the Bible requires of us as disciples: "passionate", "radical", "zealous". The triangle diagram on the following page depicts the three relationships and the arrows around it show the flow of love and grace through these relationships. It is as we belong to Christ in relationship with him that we share his love for his people and his love for those who are lost from his family.

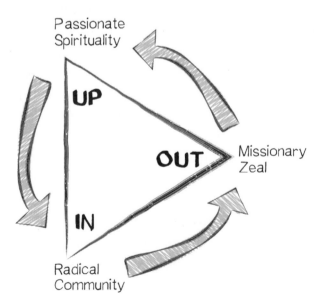

Passionate Spirituality

UP

OUT — Missionary Zeal

IN

Radical Community

Covenant: Passionate Spirituality

Covenant is our UPward relationship with God. Everything starts with God's love for us and our response to him. He is the source of love and his presence and our relationship with him is the most precious gift we will ever receive. The verse that summarises this is when Jesus says the greatest commandment is this:

"'Hear, O Israel: The Lord our God, the Lord is one. Love the Lord your God with all your heart and with all your soul and with all your mind and with all your strength.' The second is this: 'Love your neighbour as yourself.' There is no commandment greater than these.'" (Mark 12:29-31)

To have a relationship with Almighty God is unique and covenant is the word given to describe the nature of that relationship. A covenant is an agreement between a powerful party who makes a commitment to a weaker party on the basis of their acceptance of conditions of that agreement. This is the relationship which God commits to with his people in which again and again (over 15 times) he says in Scripture, *"I will be their God and they will be my people."* He was saying (long before Darth Vader did to Luke Skywalker!) "I am your Father." God is a Father and he constantly refers to us as his adopted sons and daughters. We were once without a name and outside of his family, but he chose to give us a new identity. This is the source of our significance and our freedom to live for him. We live *out of* our identity as God's children, we do not have to earn it. Jesus showed us how to live in intimate covenant relationship with his Father, abiding in him and only doing what he saw the Father doing. He teaches us to do the same and calls us to a passionate spirituality in which we love him wholeheartedly with all that we have and we enjoy him giving himself to us and filling our lives.

Community

God's desire was always to have a people for himself. So as Jesus came and opened up the opportunity for everyone to be God's son and daughter he gives them a new commandment.

"A new command I give you: Love one another. As I have loved you, so you must love one another. By this everyone will know that you are my disciples, if you love one another." (John 13:34-35)

Jesus says that it is impossible to be his disciple on our own – the solo Christian does not exist in the New Testament. Our INward relationship as a Christian community is the place where God's love and our worship of him is given expression and it is the place where the world is given a tangible demonstration of his reality. This is why in the church I lead we form Missional Communities. It is impossible to do mission on our own. The challenge in Jesus' teaching is for the quality of our love for one another to reflect his sacrificial love for us and reveal him to the world. This is *radical community*. And the connection between our loving community and mission is that the love of God in our community will be so distinctive and different that it will attract others to find out what lies at the heart of our relationships – Jesus. This is the picture we find in the description of the early Church in Acts 2:42f where they held all things in common and shared their lives together day by day.

Lesslie Newbigin writes in *The Gospel in a Pluralist Society*,

"How is it possible that the gospel should be credible, that people should come to believe that the power which has the

31

last word in human affairs is represented by a man hanging on a cross? I am suggesting that the only answer, the only hermeneutic [explanation] of the gospel, is a congregation of men and women who believe it and live by it."

This is deeply challenging to us as individualistic Western consumers, so the love of God has to do its work in us if we are to live the radical life that will reveal Jesus to others. It's not easy to love one another! As the rhyme goes,

"To live above, with the saints I love, O wouldn't that be glory. But to live below, with the saints I know, that's another story."

But when it works there is nothing like a Christian community to transform people and demonstrate the love of God. Our experience of the power of Christian community is that people outside the church love to be included in our missional communities and there are literally hundreds of them in these communities. They attend worship events, social occasions, count themselves as members and they are on a journey of faith with others. One of our missional communities has done a great job of including these "people of peace" within their worshipping and social life. Their friends would come to their BBQs, family games afternoons, all-age worship events, etc. When the community decided to go away for a weekend, one of the families who were not yet Christians said to the leader that they wanted to pay for anyone from the community who wouldn't be able to afford to go on the weekend. That family had been included within the love of that community, had experienced God's love, and were now beginning to express it, even before they had come to faith. This was their community and they had embraced its values of love and generosity.

And so we see that although these five missional practices

equip us as individuals, we need each other to create communities into which new disciples are born. As they say in Africa, it takes a village to raise a child. As we seek to make disciples, newborn babies need support, and the process of them coming to faith involves inclusion in the community even before they make that clear decision. It used to be that the order of conversion was that you Believe, then Behave, then Belong. But now it has to be, Belong, Behave (start to do things Christians do) and then you will Believe.

Another example of this is that we used to find that over 50% of people who completed the Alpha Course at Holy Trinity Church would not continue to be part of the church a year later. To address this we decided that every guest on Alpha would have a "buddy" who would include them in the life of their missional community, even while they were on Alpha (this is often their friend who invited them, but if they came on their own we would find someone from within the church who we thought would naturally "click" with them and asked them to accompany them on Alpha). At the end of Alpha they continue in that friendship and that wider community and we often baptise people within their communities because this is now their Christian family. Now we hardly lose anyone after Alpha because they haven't just formed community within Alpha, they have already been included within the community of the church.

Kingdom
This is our OUTward relationship with the world. Our Christian community cannot be inward looking and detached from those around us. If we have God's love in our hearts it will propel us outwards, out of love for those who are the

least, the last and the lost. Jesus taught us to *"Love your neighbour as yourself"* and has commissioned us to *"Go"* in his authority and make disciples (Matthew 28:19). This love is directed and moved by a compassion for the "lostness" of those who don't know Jesus. Countless people live every day with no sense of where they have come from or why they are on this planet. They live each day without the love of God for which they were created, and given the capacity to know. Instead, they try to fill that gap with things which, while often good in themselves, will never satisfy. They don't know the God-given purpose for which they were made, so they struggle on, trying to find meaning and fulfilment. And ultimately they are in danger of spending eternity excluded from heaven and separated from God in hell. How can we fail to feel compassion for people in such a state? And yet we do.

When I was in theological college, I became convicted about my lack of compassion and so when it came to the opportunity to write a dissertation I wrote 25,000 words about the decline in the belief in hell and spent many moments weeping over my keyboard.

The good news is that you don't have to do anything as extreme as writing a dissertation to address this issue, but it is vital that we recover such compassion, because it is God's love that will fuel and strengthen us in all the challenges and knock-backs of this missionary calling.

I prayed for someone in our church recently to recapture this compassion and he was deeply moved by God. As we finished praying together he expressed a fear that he would lose it again. I explained that, like all relationships and experiences of love, it will naturally ebb and flow, but if he paid attention to it, he could use some of the ways I have found to nurture a heart that is moved by such compassion.

The first is to ask the Father to give you his heart for his lost children, or for a particular person you know. Asking him to show you how he loves them can melt the hardest of hearts.

Secondly, take time to meditate on the cross of Christ. Remember its cruelty and pain. Remember that Jesus chose to go to the cross freely. Allow this to reveal how much God loves us, and to understand that it is so serious to be separated from God that he would send his own Son to the cross for us.

Finally, ask the Holy Spirit to come and release in you fresh love and desire to share the Gospel as he did for those first disciples.

Paul explained it this way:

"For Christ's love compels us, because we are convinced that one died for all, and therefore all died." (2 Corinthians 5:14)

And so God's love not only nurtures us, it propels us outwards with the sense of being sent by Jesus as his missionaries. This is missionary zeal. This "sentness" is so easily lost and yet it is integral to what it means to be the Church. The Church is apostolic in its foundations (Ephesians 2:20) and an apostle is "a sent one". The foundations of a building define its shape and what can be built upon them. In the same way, the missionary call to go is meant to define the Church. Too easily our Christian lives revert to only upward and inward relationships and become increasingly insular. We are to "go" and have a sense of being sent, even while our job, home, family circumstances remain the same. This sense is not easy to maintain. That is why the triangle in our diagram is shown on its side, with the outward point forming the point of an arrow, directing us outwards. Unless we frame all of our other relationships within the call to love others and see the kingdom come we will lose this defining aspect of the Church.

The great South African evangelist Reinhard Bonnke suggests that Jesus has designed church congregations to be like a Lifeboat Ship – out in seas ready to launch lifeboats and rescue people who are lost at sea. In a film he created called "Lost at Sea" he parodies the Church that loves to teach and talk about mission without actually doing it. In one scene, a couple of seamen, dressed in dinner jackets and bow ties, talk about lifeboat manuals, how to rescue people from stormy seas and the best practice, until one of them asks the other, "Have you actually been out to sea in a lifeboat?" And he hadn't!

UP IN & OUT together

Once we have understood all of this we allow the Holy Spirit to begin to direct and lead us in the interplay between these three relationships – because it is the interconnectedness of them that allows us to live a life of mission healthily. God's love for us, and the love we have for him, allows his love to fill our hearts for one another and for people who are lost. As we pray for them we allow God to speak to us about them. The love we have for God and one another becomes attractive if we express it in a way that enables those who are outside the Christian community to begin to experience it. So mission stops being an added extra, something separate for those who are keen, and becomes integral to our lives as disciples. As it has been said, "It is not the Church of God that has a mission, but the God of mission who has a Church."

The mission field is no longer located somewhere else,

overseas. Instead it surrounds us on every side. God's people need to be empowered as agents of the kingdom and the king. We need to learn how to think as missionaries.Furthermore, we need to develop skills that will help us meaningfully engage people and places. These skills involve learning how to better identify and participate in God's activity "out there" in our neighbourhoods, in our workplaces, and the public spaces we inhabit.

PRESS PAUSE

Before you move on to the next chapter why not stop and reflect on the love of God for you and how you are responding to the three relationships of love that we are called to. Which is strongest? Which is weakest? Where do you need to ask God to work afresh in your life?

Chapter 2
Missional Discipleship?

In 2009 I was filling in my application form for the job of Vicar of Holy Trinity Leicester. It was the standard Church of England application form which includes the question, "What is the biggest challenge facing the Church today?" I answered "discipleship – the challenge of rediscovering what it means to live as a disciple of Jesus Christ today." Later I was encouraged to discover that Dallas Willard, one of the clearest thinkers on this aspect of the Christian faith, agreed with me:

"The greatest issue facing the world today, with all its heart-breaking needs, is whether those who, by profession or culture, are identified as 'Christians' will become disciples – students, apprentices, practitioners – of Jesus Christ, steadily learning from him how to live the life of the Kingdom of the Heavens into every corner of human existence." (*The Great Omission: Reclaiming Jesus' Essential Teachings on Discipleship*).

The danger is that we think our current version of being a Christian is the correct one. Why is this dangerous? The Church in the West has lost its missional consciousness and yet the Bible is clear that the identity of the Church is fundamentally missional. So if we have forgotten our missional self-understanding as disciples of Jesus and, at the same time, believe that we are fulfilling Jesus' call without being active in mission, this will prevent us from being able to see that we have anything to learn.

The recovery of what a life of being on mission with Jesus looks like is key to the future of the Church in the West. I was sitting on a Diocesan committee a few years ago when a senior member of the clergy said, "Why is everyone obsessed with discipleship now? I just don't understand where it has come from. It used to be OK to simply believe God is on his throne, go to church on a Sunday, read the service and go home. All this talk about discipleship just makes people feel guilty." This was said without apology or fear of offending anyone – we have so much to recover.

I realise that this is all very "big picture", but this is the air that we have been breathing, the environment that has shaped our Christian formation. And it is the example we have been given to copy. Your decision to begin to practice using patterns and rhythms of missional life will involve swimming against this tide. But your decision will also help to turn the tide that I sense the Spirit is turning and will not just equip you, it will be an example to the Christian community around you.

The Greek word *mathetes,* used over 250 times in the New Testament, which we translate as "disciple", literally means "learner, student or apprentice". I like the idea of an apprentice, because it carries the idea of on-the-job training. This is in stark contrast to the passive experience that we have made following Jesus, in which discipleship is reduced to attending church on a Sunday or completing a discipleship course. This is nothing like the process of discipleship that Jesus took his disciples on.

"The Church in the West has lost its missional consciousness and yet the Bible is clear that the identity of the Church is fundamentally missional."

As someone has said, "You will never grow in a row. Only vegetables grow in rows." In other words, you can't grow as a disciple simply by sitting and listening, you need to actively learn on the job, on mission with God's people as they actively follow Jesus. Let's look at Jesus' methods.

Like other rabbis of his day, Jesus had disciples called *talmidim*. The disciples' deepest desire was to follow their rabbi so closely that they would start to think and act like him. The tradition of the day was that gifted students approached a rabbi and asked, "May I follow you?". In other words, "Do I have what it takes to be like you?" The rabbi either accepted the student as a talmid or sent him away to pursue a trade if he didn't think he was good enough. Jesus broke this pattern when he chose his own talmidim. He asked his disciples to follow him and many of those had already failed to make the grade as talmid material. The implication of him choosing young men who were fishing in their father's boat was that they had gone through the Jewish education system and not been chosen by other rabbis. This is good news for us! He chose ordinary people like you and me, not the cream of the crop, and said to them "You're just the kind of person I want to follow me."

A talmid followed the rabbi everywhere, often without knowing or asking where he was going. He rarely left his rabbi's side for fear that he would miss a teachable moment. And he watched the rabbi's every move, noting how he acted and thought about a variety of situations: how he cleaned his teeth, drank from his cup, ate his food. More seriously, we see the disciples watching Jesus pray. As they witnessed the depth of his relationship with the Father, they came to him and said, *"Lord, teach us to pray"* (Luke 11:1).

Discipleship is the process of becoming like Jesus. As C.S. Lewis wrote, "Every Christian is to become a little Christ. The whole purpose of becoming a Christian is simply nothing else." So when one of Jesus' followers came to write his description of the Christian faith, he described this experience of being with Jesus:

"That which was from the beginning, which we have heard, which we have seen with our eyes, which we have looked at and our hands have touched – this we proclaim concerning the Word of life. The life appeared; we have seen it and testify to it, and we proclaim to you the eternal life, which was with the Father and has appeared to us." (1 John 1:1-2).

John doesn't just write about Jesus' teaching as he describes Jesus, he recalls how they *saw*, they *touched*, they *shared* Jesus' life – and now they are trying to proclaim and live out this eternal life. It was this experience of sharing life with Jesus that now informed how the disciples lived out their faith in him. So we see that the life we are trying to live is *caught* and not just *taught*.

Being a disciple of Jesus at the time when he walked on the earth was costly. It meant leaving everything behind and literally following him around the Galilean countryside. It was an "all or nothing" decision. But it did have the advantage of simplicity. There was no college timetable to follow, no family life to balance, no job to fit in alongside following Jesus – a disciple simply had to follow him observe, obey, imitate and try to become more like him. Imagine how our friends, family and colleagues would react if we simply walked out of our home, our workplace, and started trying to copy Jesus, forsaking all such distractions. That isn't what Jesus is asking us to do today.

For us today the principles are the same, but there is a complexity. I wake up each day with a family to care for, a job to do and household to manage. *What does it mean for me to follow Jesus in the midst of all of this?* It is not about trying to recreate exactly what we read in the Gospels, it is more about asking "What would I do if I had Jesus' heart in me?" Again, Dallas Willard nails it for us: "Discipleship is the process of becoming who Jesus would be if he were me." Being a disciple is having Jesus' heart, his love, his presence, guiding and ruling over all I am and all I do – so that I carry the kingdom of heaven, Jesus' rule, into every place I go.

The phrase "missional discipleship" is really a tautology (a statement in which a word or idea is unnecessarily repeated because they both mean the same thing). In other words, you can't be a fully devoted disciple of Jesus without being missional. The reason the word missional has been added is because we have somehow managed to separate mission from discipleship and reduced discipleship to attending a course or studying the Bible. As Tony Pullin writes, "Discipleship doesn't come after mission – discipleship *is* our mission."

My friend Steve Addison uses the helpful analogy of a coin to describe how discipleship and mission cannot be separated. On one side of our coins we have the Queen's head as a reminder that she is sovereign and ruler over the United Kingdom. On the reverse we have the value of the coin, which the Bank of England promises to honour the value of. To try and separate these two sides of the same coin would be ridiculous. It would devalue the whole coin.

When Jesus called his first disciples he said, *"Come, follow me and I will teach you how to fish for people"* (Mark 1:17).

The call to follow him is a call to make him Lord and obey him. He immediately joins that call with a promise that he will teach us how to reach people for him. Mission is intrinsically part of following Jesus. If we really understand this call then this will give us great hope – Jesus understands that we will have to learn how to do this. We're not the finished article, but he promises to teach us, to shape our lives into patterns and practices by which we will bring others into his kingdom.

Just as those fishermen had to learn how to read the tides and weather patterns and behaviour of fish in Galilee, so Jesus would take them on a journey of discipleship in which they would learn how to do what he did. The call to follow and make him Lord is inextricably joined to the promise and priority of making disciples.

From this flows a very challenging question: *can we really be said to be following Jesus if we are not intentionally seeking to lead others to follow him?* As Christians, we can belong to Christ, experience his love, trust in his gift of eternal life, and seek to live our lives according to his values and moral teachings, but can we genuinely call ourselves a disciple of Jesus if we are not "on mission" with him? I don't think so. The good news is that all we have to do is acknowledge this and trust in the promise that Jesus will teach us to fish for people.

I wonder when the last time was that you learned something new? As we become adults, learning a new skill becomes much harder the older we get. The early years of our lives were characterised by learning and the process was always the same: try, fail, try again, get better, fail, try again, get better... I remember encouraging my youngest daughter, Alice, to walk. She was never very keen to do this in her early years.

So Bridget and I would sit across the room from one another. Bridget would hold Alice up by her hands and steady her on her feet. Then I would call to her: "Over here, Alice, come to Daddy" with a big smile and outstretched arms, encouraging her to walk. Alice would start to toddle very unsteadily towards me. She would manage a couple of steps, but before she reached me would often wobble and fall down.

How did we react? With disappointment and frustration, saying, "Oh no, we've got a 'non-walker', we had better start making plans to help Alice cope with life without being able to walk"? Of course not! I scooped her up in my arms and said, "Well done Alice, great try. Up you get, don't worry, let's try again."

In the Church we have developed strategies and patterns to help Christians follow Jesus without being involved in mission. We have got stuck in this place because the first time, or last time, we tried to share our faith with someone it didn't go well and after a few attempts we have concluded that we are just one of those disciples who can't share our faith.

The church pastor and author Jordan Seng's definition of faith is spelt T.R.Y. Jesus only challenges people about their lack of faith when they fail to TRY to do what he is calling them to. The biggest distance in the world is from thinking about doing something to actually trying it. Psychologists identify this as the "attitude–behaviour gap", where what we believe is not reflected in our behaviour. Some in the church need an attitude change – we need to recapture a desire to see those we love and share our lives with come to faith in Jesus Christ. Most Christians I know would express a desire for this to happen – but when you look at their lives and behaviour there is nothing they do which reflects this belief.

The question then is, "What is the barrier?" and in the final chapter of this book we will look at the attitude-behaviour gap and where you personally might be stuck. Having been involved in training others in disciple-making I am convinced it is often because we don't know where to start and or how to begin to try something.

These missional practices give you some things to TRY. I almost want to say, don't keep reading unless you are willing to commit to trying something new, and to persist even when it doesn't go well. As Robert the Bruce, hiding from English pursuers in a cave, was inspired to say by a humble spider struggling to weave its web, "Try, try and try again."

As adult Christians we have to be willing to try and fail and try again. The development of a culture within our churches that can manage failure and disappointment well is also important, because each attempt brings understanding of how to do the work of mission God has called us to.

James Joyce wrote, "Mistakes are the portals of discovery." Mistakes show us what we need to learn, every scientist knows this. History is littered with the statistics of how many failed experiments it took before someone made their breakthrough discovery – from Thomas Edison who made 1,000 unsuccessful attempts at inventing the light bulb, to Henry Ford who went broke 5 times before establishing the Ford motor car, and more recently (and perhaps less significantly!) James Dyson, who spent 15 years creating 5,126 versions of his Dual Cyclone vacuum cleaner that failed before he made one that worked. What was key to all of these was a determination to keep going until they succeeded and a refusal to see failure as an indicator that they would not succeed.

These are human examples of faith. When we apply this

to the challenge to make a disciple (and not a vacuum cleaner!), I hope we see this call as much more significant and something that we have to commit to until we see it happen. And I hope we apply the lessons we learn from unsuccessful attempts and continue to experiment. I am excited to see a culture of experimentation developing within the Church at this time, as we try fresh ways to introduce the good news of Jesus to people. But I wonder if, on a personal level, we have committed to allow Jesus to teach us how he will use us to make another disciple and to keep going until we do?

I like the phrase, "If a thing's worth doing, it's worth doing badly." Yes, I know we should try to do things as well as we can to honour God and permission to fail is not an excuse for lack of effort and low standards. But a culture of excellence can disempower people from trying, because the "experts'" level of performance is out of reach for us mere mortals.

The opposite of a culture of experimentation is a culture of expertise, where teacher knows best. Too often that is what church leaders and clergy have created. My favourite moments of our church's life are when we let people have a go for the first time. An 18-year old intern preaches for the first time, or a 9-year old prays alongside an adult in our healing prayer team, or the person who asks for and receives the gift of tongues and for the first time uses it, aged 80. Could I do a better job than them because of my greater experience? Of course I could, but my experience should not be a barrier to their involvement. Instead it should provide the support for them to have a go and grow through training and experience. The most encouraging thing about the Gospels is how many times the disciples blew it. Jesus challenges them, but he never gives up on them. We can imagine our Father and the great cloud of witnesses saying, "Well done, great try. Up you get, let's try again."

Jesus created a "community of practice" for three years with his twelve disciples, in which he shared his life with them and guided their growth in and understanding of the kingdom mission he'd called them to. *So how did Jesus teach his friends to be his disciples?* I have found Mike Breen's analysis of Jesus' disciple-making process helpful, in which he summarises it as having three elements: *Information*, *Imitation* and *Innovation*.

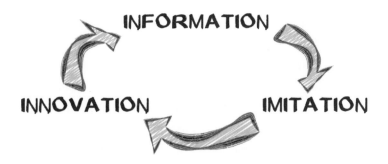

Information

We need good theology and a strong biblical foundation for our lives. Jesus taught about the kingdom of God for three years and clearly communicated the truth about God that his followers needed. Jesus was clear that we need to build our lives on his word and when we do, it becomes a rock for our lives. But as he gave this illustration he said,

"Therefore everyone who hears these words of mine and puts them into practice is like a wise man who built his house on the rock." (Matthew 7:24)

In other words, it is only the word that we *obey* that becomes the foundation of our lives. The implication is that those of us who just receive information without acting on it are building sandcastles with our lives. Within the Church today we have created an environment that almost celebrates listening to the word and doing nothing in response to it. We hope that people will listen to the sermon every Sunday and apply it to their lives, but there is often no opportunity to demonstrate a response while we are together. Instead, implicit permission is given for this response to be a private affair and no support in applying it during the week ahead is offered. Too easily we collect information and it makes us feel better about ourselves and our faith. We have aped our education system, which teaches us lots of information that we never do anything with. I learned the whole Periodic Table in my chemistry lessons, and could explain what chemical reactions would take place when certain elements were mixed, but I have never done anything with that information since. Similarly, we have bred disciples who are consumers of teaching, and taught them to demand more and more information without applying what they have already heard. I think this requires a change of attitude in our teaching. Just appropriating information is not what God is calling us to.

One of the results of this approach is that people are weak in faith because they are not used to trusting the truth of God's word as they step out on it. Jesus says that it is only the word that we trust in, put our weight on and live out in our lives that becomes like a foundational rock in our lives. Simply giving intellectual assent to biblical truth is not enough.

As we engage with living missionally, it is an opportunity to develop new patterns of responding to God's word and strengthen our faith. This is all about obedience to Jesus Christ, who says that we will be his witnesses and calls us to be ready to give an account for the hope within us. We are called to obey our Lord's commands and when we do he promises us that such obedience will establish our lives on him. When we share our testimony and choose to be witnesses it strengthens our faith; it speaks to our spirit that we have been saved; that we are followers of Jesus and we are living for him. This sets off a spiritual momentum within our lives. When a friend comes to faith in Jesus and he transforms their life, we are strengthened again to believe that the Gospel really is "the power of God to save those who believe". And sadly, the opposite is true. If we live as a Christian without stepping out in faith, and without experiencing God use us to bless and reach others, our faith begins to diminish, to whither like unpicked fruit on the vine.

James writes in his letter,

"Do not merely listen to the word, and so deceive yourselves. Do what it says. Anyone who listens to the word but does not do what it says is like someone who looks at his face in a mirror and, after looking at himself, goes away and immediately forgets what he looks like. But whoever looks intently into the perfect law that gives freedom and continues in it – not forgetting what they have heard but doing it – they will be blessed in what they do." (James 1:22-25)

In the model Jesus demonstrates of training his disciples, there is never a moment recorded when they sit down together to study Scripture. *Why is that?* I think it is because when they were with him, he was the living word and he was constantly teaching them. And this teaching and feeding on God's word took place within a context of mission. They were always on the move. Jesus was giving them new experiences and challenges and teaching them in these moments of apprenticeship.

So now that he is not physically with us we need to read, and learn and feed on Scripture, and allow the Holy Spirit to speak to us, teach us and lead us to apply it. But we need to do this within the context of mission like the disciples. Having a Bible study isn't the goal of our faith, rather Scripture is the doorway to our relationship with our mission leader, Jesus. It is food for our journey; light to guide our path as we follow him on mission. We are called to live holy lives and to be holy as our heavenly Father is holy (1 Peter 1:16). Holy means "set apart" and it is vital our lives reflect God, the one to whom we are devoted. But we have been set apart for a God who has called us to fulfil his purpose, which is to bring his kingdom on earth and reconcile a world back to himself. In other words, mission is not an added extra for the keen ones after we have repented of sin and lived holy lives. Mission is being set apart for a missionary God who has called us to follow him.

My hope is that through these missional practices you will be able to begin to actively obey Jesus' call to make others his disciples and discover the blessing that comes through obedience. We need information, good biblical teaching, but then we need to live it out. Most of us already have more than enough information to be dangerous in God's kingdom. It's not the bits of the Bible that I don't understand that bother me, it's the ones I do understand, because if I obeyed them they would turn my life upside down! I have a saying: "You haven't learned anything until you have done it." There has to be a change in our behaviour. We don't have to have done it very *well*, we just have to have tried. We need good biblical teaching, but the question is whether we will do anything with what God has taught us?

As a church, when we moved to missional communities

we reduced the time given to Bible study in small groups and gave missional communities the encouragement to meet in their own communities for Sunday worship at least once per month. I had a number of people bring concerns to me about us devaluing the preaching of the word and what would happen as a result of this. I took these concerns seriously, but my response was to say that we were actually valuing the word of God more highly, because we were creating structures and rhythms of life that would allow people to be active in mission and actively discipling one another, rather than sitting in rows listening to the word but not doing anything with it. How do we honour God and his word? By obeying it.

Imitation

Clarence Day said, "Information's pretty thin stuff unless mixed with experience." Jesus knew this and mixed his teaching within a process of training and disciple-making that was all about sharing his life with his disciples and them imitating his example. This is an essential element of discipleship: copying what others have found works.

Paul knew it too as he wrote, *"Imitate me as I imitate Christ"* (1 Corinthians 11:1). Jesus really was the greatest leader that this world has ever experienced. He knew how to mentor and invest in his followers in such a way that when he returned to heaven, and the Holy Spirit filled them, they turned their world upside down. They are the missional disciples that we have to imitate.

As human beings we naturally learn by copying. Children imitate sounds as they start to speak. They might pick up the TV remote control and pretend to be on the telephone. They intuitively pick up the latest technology, swiping touch screens as they imitate adults without any understanding of what they are doing. Even though I am right handed, I hold my pen like a left-handed person, because my primary school teacher Miss Adams was left handed. She tried to stop me doing this, but I was determined to copy her due to my schoolboy crush! But when you look at how we help new Christians grow in faith, the idea of sharing our lives with them and them imitating our Christian practice is almost completely absent from our churches.

At Holy Trinity we ask established Christians to disciple new believers. This is not just in how to read the Bible and pray, but in being filled with the Holy Spirit and sharing faith and making other disciples. On a number of occasions we have had olders Christian come to us and say, "There is a problem. I'm not actually doing what I am being asked to help the new Christian do!" This is the church's problem in a nutshell. We are presenting a distorted picture of what it means to follow Jesus and others are copying it. The picture we give of Christian discipleship is to "attend a worship service in a building led by a professional Christian, read the Bible and pray personally, and attend a small group (only if you are one of the keen ones!) where we study the Bible and pray." In effect we have all been copying the wrong pattern. We have been discipled within a Church culture that has lost confidence in mission and we keep on copying it.

There is a story about a man on a building site who was asked by his foreman to cut eighty planks of wood to board the outside of a house. The foreman cut the first plank to size and said, "Produce eighty more like that." The workman cut the first one, but then used the second plank as the pattern for the third and so on. By the time he reached his eightieth plank it was over a foot shorter than the original. Each reproduction had copied the flaw of the previous one.

This is why we need to address the issue of imitation so seriously. We have been copying Christians from previous generations who have reproduced a flawed picture of what a disciple looks like.

In the New Testament three words are used for our English word "example":

- *Hupogrammos* – an exact written copy (1 Peter 2:21)
- *Mimeomal* – to imitate or model the faith of others (2 Thessalonians 3:7-9)
- *Tupos* – to make a stamp (1 Timothy 4:12)

They all carry the meaning of reproducing the characteristics of the original model. So we have to pay attention to the model we have been set and we have to proactively decide to choose to follow a different model where we recognise its limitations. Otherwise, we will keep reproducing the wrong example of discipleship in our lives. When we look at the kind of disciples Jesus produced, we see in the early Church a community on mission with the Holy Spirit empowering and leading them. They took opportunities to share the Gospel, heal the sick, drive out demons and see God's love and power transform people and whole communities. If that is not the kind of disciples we are producing I don't think its unreasonable to suggest that we are copying the wrong example! And the big question I have to ask myself is, "Is my Christian life worth copying?"

But as well as regaining the right pattern to copy, we also have to regain the tools of disciple-making. What did Jesus do to apprentice his disciples? He used the classic process of:

- *Model*: I do – you watch
- *Assist*: I do – you help
- *Watch*: You do – I help
- *Leave*: You do – I support

When Jesus left his disciples and ascended to heaven we then see how they followed his examples. In Acts 3 when Peter and John were walking to the temple they see the lame man who asks them for money. Peter says, "Get up and walk" and takes the man's hand, helping him to his feet. I wonder where we have seen that before? (Jesus with the paralysed man who was lowered through the roof in Mark 2:41). When Peter is faced with the death of Tabitha and all the widows are wailing and mourning her death in Acts 9, he clears them out of the room and then says to Tabitha, "Get up" in an exact repetition of how Jesus raises Jairus' daughter from the dead (Mark 5:41-42). I don't imagine Jesus running "This is how you heal a lame person" or "This is how you raise the dead" classes. He just took his disciples with him and they got it. He then gave them a chance to try and fail while he was with them. In the same way, we have to create relationships in which experienced Christians model this life to new believers.

So who can provide that good example of what living like a missional disciple looks like? The aim of the second section of this book is to give practical suggestions and examples that we can begin to copy, to try out to get us moving forward. It also explains how one-to-one mentoring and shared lives in community are key to giving examples for others to follow and creating a culture of learning together.

Innovation

A musical analogy to illustrate this is jazz. How do you explain jazz music? Improvisation is the key element of jazz. It is partly planned and partly spontaneous. That is, as the musicians perform a pre-determined tune, they have the opportunity to create their own interpretations within that tune in response to the other musicians' performances and whatever else may occur. In other words, individual musicians have the freedom to express themselves on their instrument, as long as they maintain their responsibility to the other musicians by adhering to the overall framework and structure of the tune.

The famous jazz saxophonist Stan Getz said,

"It's like a language. You learn the alphabet, which are the scales. You learn sentences, which are the chords. And then you talk extemporaneously with the horn. It's a wonderful thing to speak extemporaneously, which is something I've never gotten the hang of. But musically I love to talk just off the top of my head. And that's what jazz music is all about."

Each of us is unique. God has placed us in unique situations and we all have different spiritual gifts, personalities and experiences. Yet, at the same time, we are all called to be witnesses. So under the Holy Spirit's empowering and guidance we have to innovate with the missional tools and express them in ways that work for us and produce the fruit God wants to through our lives. The "Calling" aspect of *Mission-Shaped Grace* in Section 2 explores this in greater depth. So my prayer is that you will receive these practices as tools to improvise with – musical notes or colours on a pallette – and that the Holy Spirit will lead and inspire you to play and paint the kingdom into the world where God has placed.

After three years Jesus left his disciples and said that the

Holy Spirit would guide them as they applied all that they had learned. They then had to innovate under the Spirit's guidance in order to respond to the different situations they faced. And so we see the kingdom coming as the early Church develops new patterns of life and mission which we find described in Paul, Peter and John's letters.

That is what we are called to do today. And a key reason that innovation is vital is the unique context in which we find ourselves in the West. As I have suggested already, the previous generations have failed to produce a Church confident in mission and relevant to the world around us. Something has to change. But we are also in a really different cultural context. Our post-modern culture is not generally asking "Is this true?" because they have rejected any absolute truth and are free to define truth for themselves. But what they *are* looking for is "What works?"

This is why these missional practices will enable you to look for opportunities to demonstrate the reality of God and his love for people – healing the sick, ministering his presence to someone, telling stories of faith, as well as faithfully loving and serving them. I also think that because our culture has rejected organised religion, and has a distrust of institution, then the ability of Christians to live a relevant and authentic life of faith that reveals Jesus to those around them is even more important. No longer will an invitation to a church meeting do the job. If we are going to reach people who no one else has reached we are going to have to innovate and do things that no one else has done before.

PRESS PAUSE

Take some time to reflect on your experience of being a disciple since you came to faith in Jesus. Does it reflect some of the distortions presented in this chapter? How willing are you to allow God to teach you a different way of being Jesus' disciple today? How willing are you to offer an example for others to follow and would you want others to imitate you?

Chapter 3
What Would Jesus Do?

If we are trying to find a "plank" to copy from Jesus' practice of mission, the story of him sending out the 72 disciples into local villages ahead of him visiting them is a great example. Take a moment to read Luke 10:1-9. The *Mission-Shaped Grace* practices connect with many of the principles that Jesus trains his disciples in here. The significance of this account in Luke's Gospel is that it is a repeat of the training he gives to the twelve disciples who he sends out in chapter 9. Whenever something is repeated in Scripture we need to take notice. I don't think it is unreasonable to conclude that Luke is describing a pattern that Jesus repeated a number of times as he trained his disciples in mission.

In between the two accounts in Luke 9 and 10, Luke reports on Jesus multiplying food to feed the five thousand and the cost of discipleship. So the move from the twelve to the seventy-two can be seen as a picture of the ever-expanding nature of disciple-making. Involvement in Jesus' mission is not the preserve of the elite twelve apostles, but of a wider group of seventy-two of Jesus' followers and beyond. This breaks down any argument that it is only the original twelve apostles who were special enough to heal the sick, pronounce blessings and announce the kingdom.

Since the expansion of the kingdom has now reached us, it is good to go back to look at what "Jesus-shaped mission" looked like. Here are eight qualities of missional disciples that we can take from this passage:

1. Hopeful

"The harvest is plentiful, but the workers are few. Ask the Lord of the harvest, therefore, to send out workers into his harvest field." (Luke 10:2)

One of the lies that we have swallowed as Jesus' followers today is that people aren't interested in God and faith. As soon as we begin to think about sharing faith with others we immediately anticipate rejection and a breaking of relationship or loss of reputation with someone. Jesus begins by saying, *"The harvest is plentiful, but the workers are few..."* Jesus says the problem isn't that people are not ready to respond to him, the problem is that there are too few people actively involved in harvesting.

To address this question in Leicester we organised a week of mission with a team from the mission agency MOVE. We set out to visit as many homes in different areas of Leicester as we could. In the mornings, Steve and Michelle Addison and their team trained people in many of the practices included in the *Grace Notes* material. Then in the afternoons and evenings we visited people in their homes. We ended up training about 80 people, and then found 1500 homes who answered the door to us. We simply said, "Hi, we're from a local church and we're walking round the neighbourhood asking people what we can pray for them. What could we pray for you?" Of the 1500, approximately 500 people allowed us to pray with them. Some of them were just being polite and weren't assertive enough to say "no", but others were very genuine. People were moved to tears, some came to genuine faith, others invited us back to share Bible stories with them. But the point of the story is this: the fields are ready for harvest and we now know that, on average, one third of people in Leicester are open to us praying with them. The issue is not people's openness, but our willingness to go. So don't say people's "no's" for them. In other words, don't talk yourself out of inviting, or asking someone if you can pray for them, or sharing your story with them because you expect them to say "no". Ask the question and let them decide how they want to respond.

2. Vulnerable

"I am sending you out like lambs among wolves. Do not take a purse or bag or sandals; and do not greet anyone on the road." (Luke 10:3)

I imagine those seventy-two disciples getting ready for their mission trip. Jesus has called them together, ready to be sent out on mission. They have arrived for the mission launch with their rucksacks packed with a spare pair of sandals, a change of underwear, maps of the local area, money to cover the cost of food and accommodation etc, and Jesus begins his training session with: *"Go! ... do not take a purse or bag or sandals; and do not greet anyone on the road."*

"Drop your bags," Jesus says, "you're not allowed to take anything with you. And by the way, you are going to face some serious opposition. You'll feel like lambs walking into wolf territory."

What is Jesus doing? He is explaining that mission involves making ourselves vulnerable as we step out of our comfort zone. He is calling his disciples to take a risk, to trust him and to go on an adventure for him. He wants them to discover that they are able to do more than they ever thought or imagined possible; to have an experience of the kingdom coming through their hands that they could never have if they played it safe.

It reminds me of the advert Ernest Shackleton is reported to have placed in London newspapers in the early 1900s for his Antarctica Expedition:

"Men wanted for hazardous journey. Low wages, bitter cold, long hours of complete darkness. Safe return doubtful. Honour and recognition in event of success."

There is something of risk and adventure that is meant to characterise our following of Jesus. We may not be called to travel to the South Pole, but as Bill Hybels has said, we are called to "walk across the room" and bring God's presence and the Gospel to others.

You are a missionary, because a missionary isn't someone who crosses the sea but someone who sees the cross and responds to the amazing grace of Jesus Christ by taking the risk of sharing it with others. And when we do this, it gives us an opportunity to demonstrate our faith and conviction. That speaks to us too, affirming the fact that we do belong to Christ and we are living for him. In feeling the fear and vulnerability, but doing it anyway, our faith comes alive and feels more real and tangible.

I wonder when was the last time you were involved in mission and you felt the fear but did it anyway? I remember when I was part of a team preparing to take the Jesus Video door to door in a previous parish. The trainer said, "I'm going to separate you into two groups. Those of you who are scared meet over here and those who are absolutely terrified come with me." The fear of the unknown, of rejection, not knowing what to say, or getting it wrong were real for all of us. But our experience was the same as the first disciples when they returned. We came back excited and amazed at how positively it had gone.

So often our fears are "**F**alse **E**xpectations **A**ppearing **R**eal". The only way to overcome them is by actually doing it and becoming more confident in these practices. By acknowledging our fears and doing it anyway we express faith and we overcome fear. Our trepidation grows smaller and our faith in Jesus grows stronger.

The other aspect of the vulnerability that Jesus created was *dependency*. Dependency forces us deeper and closer in relationship. Without money or food or clothes these disciples were forced to connect with people to see who would open their home to them. Without anything to offer these people, other than the kingdom of heaven, they had to heal the sick and drive out evil spirits and declare the kingdom of God was coming near to them – and explain it was all because of Jesus. That was all they had to offer. The impossibility of the task created humility and a dependency on God.

I have found it challenging to analyse my approach to mission using the five "capitals" that each of us has to invest in any venture. The "five capitals" concept is that we all have five kinds of resource (capital) available to us: financial, intellectual, physical, relational and spiritual.

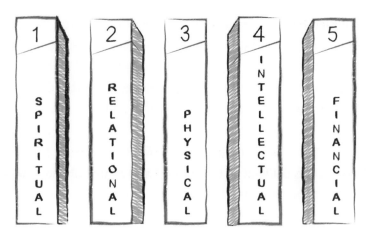

The Five Capitals

Depending on our value system we will use these capitals in different ways. In our Western culture a business would tend to prioritise them in the above order. We look for financial resources to buy property, employ staff and purchase stock. We then come up with strategic plans, forecasts, a 5-year vision etc, using our intellectual ability. We then bring that financial and intellectual capital together in physical action and ability, which is limited by our past experience, health, the size of our team and number of hours available to that task. We might then take time to manage relationships and, if we are Christians, we might pray and seek to use the spiritual principles of work, rest, love and grace to shape the delivery of our project. *The problem with this is that it is the complete opposite of Jesus' approach!*

Jesus' very incarnation was an example of vulnerability in mission. Born as a baby dependent on his parents, he spent 30 years in obscurity and faithful obedience to his heavenly Father and earthly family. Then, as God called him to begin his public ministry, he started by investing spiritually. The

Spirit led him to fast for 40 days in the wilderness and when he returned from this in the power of the Spirit, he quoted Isaiah 61:

"The Spirit of the sovereign Lord is upon me because he has anointed me to..."

He then took time to invest relationally as he called the twelve disciples to him and he invested so much of his time in them. It is only out of this spiritual and relational investment that he then directed his mission team to reach every village in Galilee (physical and intellectual capitals) and finances were kept to a minimum.

Jesus' way of doing mission was dependent on the Holy Spirit's power and on his team – a prioritisation of the spiritual and relational. *Grace Notes* is based on the principle that ordinary believers, on mission with each other and filled with the Holy Spirit, can make disciples. We don't need a big budget or impressive events. We go out in the power of the Spirit, feeling vulnerable, but trusting in the grace of God.

Before we move away from this principle, I also think that vulnerability is key to the interactions we have with people as we talk about faith. As those seventy-two disciples knocked on doors and shared faith, they also had to explain that they had nowhere to stay and no relatives in that village ready to give them a bed for the night. I imagine them being careful not to offend people and humble in their request for help.

In the past, churches' evangelistic campaigns and approaches have sometimes betrayed an arrogance in us. Sometimes this has shown up in a focus on sin and the Church appears judgmental and "holier than thou". At other times it has been through overly slick, confident presentations that sound like marketing pitches.

Instead, it can be helpful to understand that our vulnerability and weaknesses do not disqualify us, but are actually a gift. When we can't answer all of a person's questions or refute their arguments, or we are aware of some of the failings of our life that our friend knows about, we stop trying to prove our point and simply come back to our testimony. And our vulnerability and inability to give slick answers is a gift to the other person, because they now see that we haven't got everything sorted, yet we are still convinced of one thing – that Jesus is the Saviour of the world and following him is the best way to live this life.

Our culture is looking for authenticity, so admitting your faults and limitations, but still being willing to share Jesus with others, is very powerful. It reminds me of a friend of mine, Tim, whom God has set free significantly from a phobia of eating many foods. He works in the building trade, a very macho environment. Wherever he goes he tells his testimony of how Jesus has set him free, but says that he still has some issues that he is working through. Recently, he was at an industry event where he shared his testimony with two guys from another firm. They immediately started to tell him about their vulnerability in terms of relationship issues and depression and the conversation went to deeper levels, all because of Tim risking being vulnerable with them.

One description of evangelism is "one beggar helping another beggar to find bread." Our vulnerability places us on the same level as those we are sharing with and counters any sense of being the clever or holier or better ones.

Available: being sent
"Go! I am sending you." (Luke 10:3)

Within the Western Church we have replaced the word "Go" with "Come". Our evangelistic strategy is one of invitation – to a church service, an evangelistic event, or to an Alpha Course at which a professional Christian will do the job of bringing our friend to faith. This has many good aspects, but only if it sits within the wider understanding of evangelism. As others have said, there is a "Go" in the Gospel. The Gospels and the book of Acts paint a clear picture of people being "sent" or going. The apostolic nature of the Church means that we are corporately a *sent* people.

One of the challenges in this for us is how to express our "sentness" within the daily pattern of our lives, which is rightly focused on work, family life, housing, finances, our children's education etc. This is all part of the life which God calls us to see his kingly rule come into and transform. Yet the call to be witnesses, to be missional disciples, remains. So instead of reducing mission to professionally run evangelistic projects, let's learn how to live with a sense of being sent to the people in our family, workplace and friendship circle. That's why we need to be equipped to share faith, minister God's presence, tell stories and explain the Gospel to those we love and share our lives with.

Seeking to Bless

"When you enter a house, first say, 'Peace to this house.' If someone who promotes peace is there, your peace will rest on them; if not, it will return to you." (Luke 10:5)

I want you to imagine that a line of all the people that you meet regularly in your daily life has formed in front of you. They are all going to come and say hello to you one by one and you have to tell me which ones of them are currently open to knowing more about Jesus. How can you tell? On the surface, you can't. They all look like regular people and most of them probably haven't shown any interest in spiritual things. But it is very likely that some of them are spiritually seeking. How can I be sure about this? Because every single human being has been created for a relationship with God. As St Augustine said, "Lord, you have created us for yourself, and our souls are restless until they find their rest in you."

Now, many people manage to dull that ache and sense of a God-shaped hole in their lives by filling it with other ambitions, things, and experiences. But it never goes away and the Holy Spirit is at work out in the world, drawing people to himself and stirring up that desire for something more.

But you still don't know who that God-prepared person is. The way to discover this is to see how they respond to an experience of God's word and presence touching their lives. The challenge is that in order for this to happen, you have to *do* something!

Jesus tells us to, *"say 'peace to this house...'"* For us that might be the simple act of speaking a word of hope or testimony, or offering to pray for the person. Or it may be more direct, like explaining the Gospel or asking them if they would like to meet up to read the Bible with you. How they react will tell you whether they are a "person of peace". Many of the missional practices are tools to test the spiritual waters with a friend or colleague and to give an opportunity for God's presence to touch them.

"People of peace" language has become increasingly popular in churches looking to be more missional and it comes from this passage as a short-hand phrase to describe those who welcome us into their lives to share our faith with them. They are not just people who you are praying will become Christians. But this can easily be misunderstood, because a person of peace is not just a friend or colleague who is not yet a Christian. I'll say that again: *a person of peace is not just a friend or colleague who is not yet a Christian!* They are not people you have included on a list of 5 people you are praying will become Christians, but who live miles away from you and with whom you have no regular contact. Here is a clear definition of a "person of peace" which is consistent with the Luke 10 context:

Someone with whom you have regular contact who is not yet a Christian, and when you shared your faith with them in some way, they showed an openness which has resulted in you now able being able to actively (and appropriately) share your faith with them.

Helen was supporting her friend whose son was very ill and in intensive care at the hospital. On one hospital visit she offered to pray with her friend and for her son's recovery. Her friend was very moved by this and welcomed the offer of prayer. Helen prayed with her and soon after that prayer her son recovered. Helen now regularly talks about faith with her friend, all because she took the risk to offer prayer. It was the initial offer of prayer that revealed her friend's openness to spiritual things and that enabled ongoing conversations to take place.

Demonstrating the Kingdom

"When you enter a town and are welcomed, eat what is offered to you. Heal those there who are ill." (Luke 10:8)

Demonstrating the kingdom before we talk about it can sound scary, but it often opens people up to God in ways that words alone can't. It can be much easier to explain the good thing that God has just done in a person's life, than have to persuade them that God exists. Once Jesus has healed them they are no longer asking, "Is God real?" they will be asking, "What just happened?"

I remember one time when I was walking my dog and I saw a little old lady shuffling along. She looked in pain and it was a cold, rainy morning and I was concerned for her.

"Are you okay?" I asked her.

"Not really," she replied. "I've broken my foot and the doctor said I shouldn't walk on it, but I haven't got anyone to walk my dog."

"Could I pray for you?" I asked. "I go to church and God sometimes heals people when we pray for them."

"Do you think it will work?" she asked.

"I don't know, but I don't think it would hurt to try."

"Okay then."

At that moment my dog, who was on a lead, decided to get friendly with her dog and became entangled in her dog's lead, so I wrestled them apart one-handed whilst holding an umbrella in my other hand. This was no holy moment! I then said the simplest of prayers:

"Thank you, Lord Jesus, that you love Jean. Please heal her foot. In Jesus' name, foot be healed. Amen."

I then suggested she might see how her foot was. She put her weight on it and said,

"I can feel my toes. I can move my foot. The pain has gone!"

She then walked around a bit and tested that her foot had

indeed been healed. Jean and I talked about God loving her and then, in the coming weeks when I saw her at the park, I invited her to meet somewhere for a coffee to talk about life and faith, but she wasn't ready to do that.

What always strikes me about the Gospels and Acts is that all the miracles take place in public. They are in people's homes, on the streets, in village centres. Of course, the Holy Spirit wants to heal and set Christians free and to work among us when we meet together. But we have domesticated him – kept him caged, confined to certain times and places in our worship services. We have often also said that only certain "authorised" people can minister to others. It is appropriate that in large public gatherings people know that those who they go to for prayer are trained and will handle things in confidence. But most of our churches or small groups are small enough for us all to minister to one another. We have to break the professionalization of ministry in our churches. As John Wimber said, "We all get to play." We need to create opportunities to pray with people and heal the sick so that the meeting place is the training place for the marketplace. Our experience of praying with others in the church will build our confidence to do it with those outside the church. If we don't do it in here, we will never do it out there.

Proclaiming the Kingdom
"Jesus said 'Tell them the kingdom of God has come near.'"
(Luke 10:9)

In the 1990s I remember going to conference after conference on mission and hearing the now completely discredited quote from St Francis of Assisi: "Preach the Gospel at all times. If necessary use words." It has been proven that Francis never said those words, but we have now also discredited the sentiment of the statement. The Gospel has to be proclaimed. I understand the sentiment behind the quote, because there is the danger of us just preaching at people. But in reacting to this danger we have now swung too far the other way and unless we use words, our loving actions cannot point people to Jesus.

The term "gospel" in the New Testament is the translation of the Greek noun *euangelion* (occurring 76 times) meaning "good news" and the verb evangelize comes from *euangelizo* (occurring 54 times), meaning "to bring or announce good news." Both words are derived from the noun *angelos*, "messenger." In classical Greek, an *euangelos* was one who brought a message of victory, or other political or personal news, that caused joy. It meant "to speak as a messenger of gladness; to proclaim good news." So the sharing of the gospel, good news, of Jesus Christ has within it the call for it to be proclaimed and announced. We cannot escape this, however uncomfortable that might make us feel.

We might have some sympathy with Rebecca Pippert Manley who wrote, "Evangelism was something I didn't want to do to my dog let alone my best friend." How to speak of Jesus and how to share all that he means to us is difficult in our culture. There are so many barriers that immediately have to be overcome: people distrust organised religion, people are suspicious of others trying to impose their version of "truth" on them, and people in Western culture are often not living openly with spiritual questions and can show no evidence of any spiritual need or desire.

And yet we are called to speak of Jesus; to give the reason

for the hope that is in us. And with those who we are in long term regular friendship, we have to learn how to do this in a way that is not crass, disrespectful or off-putting. To break the sound barrier with someone with whom we have not established an openness about our faith is not easy. In the Asking Questions Telling Stories chapter I give some tips on how to have loving God-filled conversations.

In the Anglican denomination that I belong to The Five Marks of Mission established by the Anglican Church are:

- To proclaim the Good News of the kingdom
- To teach, baptise and nurture new believers
- To respond to human need by loving service
- To transform unjust structures of society, to challenge violence of every kind and pursue peace and reconciliation
- To strive to safeguard the integrity of creation, and sustain and renew the life of the earth
  (Bonds of Affection-1984 ACC-6 p49, Mission in a Broken World-1990 ACC-8 p101)

These marks are a great summary of the full mission of God in which we are involved. But what is more important about them is that they are in the right order – proclaiming the Good News of the kingdom and teaching, baptising and nurturing new believers comes first. Yes, each one of these marks should be present in every Christian community, but the capacity of Christian communities to offer loving service, fight for justice and steward creation is only to the extent that they have made disciples through proclaiming the Good News of the kingdom.

Discerning: should I stay or should I go now?

"Stay there, eating and drinking whatever they give you, for the worker deserves his wages. Do not move around from house to house ... But when you enter a town and are not welcomed, go into its streets and say, 'Even the dust of your town we wipe from our feet as a warning to you. Yet be sure of this: the kingdom of God has come near." (Luke 10:7-11)

While you try to remove the earworm of The Clash's famous song from your mind, let me open up the most important aspect of this passage: *you don't have to keep sharing the Gospel with people who aren't interested.* Isn't that the most liberating, guilt-reducing truth you've heard? And yet, we rarely explain this when we teach on evangelism. The permission to leave when the blessing is rejected is the gift of Luke recording Jesus' missional principles, because it releases us from pressure. Jesus is not asking us to keep knocking at a closed door. If someone who we offer to pray with or share a testimony with rejects it or responds indifferently, Jesus says, "You don't have to stay." It helps us to know that when people aren't interested, it isn't our failure, they are just not in a place to receive the Gospel. If this is a friend or family member, it doesn't mean that you stop praying for them or loving them. It just means for the immediate future you are released from the expectation to beat them into submission with your Bible!

I think this addresses many of the issues we can have with the pressure to evangelise. We understand the call to share the Good News, but so often it doesn't feel like good news because the other person has made it perfectly clear that they are not interested. In such situations Jesus' instructions release us from trying to force or pressurise them.

But what I find more challenging is the call to "stay". Jesus is clear that when we find a "person of peace" we are to stay with them, eat their food, and share their lives. This is challenging because it involves *time* – a reshaping of our diaries and priorities; being willing to be vulnerable and open with them.

Early on in our church's journey of establishing missional communities, most of the newly formed groups fell into the trap of running a programme of events. They would build a programme designed to reach out to their group of friends or a neighbourhood in a part of Leicester. This was done with the best of intentions, but it was also done without an understanding of what Jesus is teaching here about sharing our lives with people, not events. On one occasion when I was explaining this to someone they said, "So let me get this straight. You want me to spend time with people in between inviting them to outreach events?" It seemed a completely alien concept. Events are really helpful gathering and connecting places for people to deepen friendships and be included within Christian community, but they are not a substitute for actually sharing our lives with others. Loving and serving and being a faithful friend to someone while they go on their journey to faith is costly and sacrificial, but it's what it will take and it is what Jesus calls us to do. We will look at this again in the "Eating Together" practice in Section 2.

I remember when part of my job as a vicar was to go and record a "thought for the day" at a local independent radio broadcaster. The DJ responsible for recording this was a guy called Nick. He and I got to know each other over the months and had a number of faith-focused conversations in which Nick showed an openness. We also shared a love of Liverpool Football Club and beer, and so we spent a few evenings watching football matches in a local pub. Along the way Nick's children went to the holiday club at our church, he met and fell for a young woman in our church community, and through all of these connections Nick then accepted the invitation to come on the Alpha Course where he came to faith. It was a journey over many months and Nick's journey of discipleship continues as he is now a vicar!

Those first disciples would move on from any closed door and look for a household who would receive them. When we have shared faith or offered to pray with someone and it is rejected, it should cause us to pray, "Lord, who *have* you prepared for me to share my faith with? Who is it?" You move on, but you don't give up. The implication of the passage is that Jesus says to keep knocking until you find the person who receives your blessing and welcomes you in. I wonder if we are willing to live like this? To live with the conviction that I am called to be a witness for Jesus and to make another disciple, and until I find the God-prepared person he has put in my life, I am going to keep praying, looking and sharing. My experience is that when I am not in a friendship with someone who is open to faith, it causes me to pray persistently and makes me more missionally alert for opportunities to share. My "person of peace" antenna is constantly up.

Joyful

"The seventy-two returned with joy and said, 'Lord, even the demons submit to us in your name.' He replied, 'I saw Satan fall like lightning from heaven. I have given you authority to

trample on snakes and scorpions and to overcome all the power of the enemy; nothing will harm you. However, do not rejoice that the spirits submit to you, but rejoice that your names are written in heaven.'" (Luke 10:17-20)

I love the surprise contained in the disciples' report, "even the demons submit to us". In other words, "Lord, it worked, even for me. It actually worked!" We sometimes talk about the cost of discipleship but I like Dallas Willard's idea of the cost of non-discipleship. He says the cost of *not* living as a disciple of Jesus is missing out on, "abiding peace, living a life penetrated by love, faith that responds to every situation in a knowledge of God's goodness and his presence, that stands firm amidst discouragement, threat or pain, has the power to do good in the face of evil – the cost of non-discipleship is missing the abundant life Jesus offers."

"Joy" isn't why we get involved in mission, but it is definitely a by-product. Every time someone comes to faith there is such joy – joy because it shows the power of the Gospel, joy because we discover that we are someone who God can use to reveal himself, and joy because we love that person and we've longed for them to receive God's gift of salvation. It renews our faith and releases fresh vision and hope for mission.

We have recently been involved in a week of street evangelism. The most exciting aspect was seeing people who had never done this before coming back overflowing with joy as they had had the opportunity to pray with someone and to help that person pray and open their life up to God's love.

PRESS PAUSE

Take some time to review the 8 attitudes of disciple-making:

- Hopeful
- Vulnerable
- Available
- Seeking to bless
- Demonstrating the kingdom
- Proclaiming the kingdom
- Discerning
- Joyful

Where do you already pray and live out these attitudes? Give thanks for what God has already taught you and worked in your life. Ask for his grace to grow in attitudes where you are weaker.

"We have confused our calling with our destiny, believing that all we are called to do is wait for the day we will go to heaven.

No, our destiny is to go to heaven, but our calling is to bring heaven to earth."

Chapter 4
Who Do You Think You Are?

"Am I allowed to do this?" asked the little 80-year old lady in front of me. I had been leading a training day in some of these missional practices for a local church. I had taught people many of the principles contained in this book and explained that they had the authority to bless and pray for people. Why wasn't she convinced? Because years of church attendance had told her again and again that only certain special people (vicars) could pray blessings on people – and she wasn't one of them. I could have wept.

The BBC programme *Who Do You Think You Are?* takes celebrities on a journey into their ancestry to discover where they have come from. They are always deeply moved by the stories of their grandparents and previous generations, and it clearly impacts upon how they see themselves today and who they understand themselves to be. This is because "who we are" is determined by "whose we are" and this is never more true than for Christians.

One of the key battlegrounds over whether we will do the things Jesus commissioned his disciples to do lies between our ears. And the focus of that battle is our identity in Christ. The descriptions of Satan as *"the thief"* (John 10:10), *"the Father of lies"* (John 8:44) and *"the accuser of God's people"*

(Revelation 12:10) come together in his attack on our thinking and feelings. He attempts to rob us of our inheritance in Christ, and prevent us from fulfilling the call to represent Christ in this world. He does this by turning our negative experiences, our pain, weakness and sin, into issues about our identity that disqualify us from being people God can use in his kingdom.

Undoubtedly these realities will have an effect on us, but they do not disqualify us, because it was never our performance, ability or holiness that qualified us in the first place. The Gospel writers don't hide the moments when Jesus rebukes people – the Pharisees and his disciples most regularly. But in every instance, Jesus is never saying to the person, "You're rubbish, I condemn and reject you." What he is always doing is saying, "Why are you living like that? You're so much better than that. There is so much more potential in you than that. I'm challenging you to live differently because I know you can." I sense Jesus bringing the same challenge to his Church today.

The Genesis account of creation tells us,

"So God created mankind in his own image, in the image of God he created them; male and female he created them. God blessed them and said to them, 'Be fruitful and increase in number; fill the earth and subdue it. Rule over the fish in the sea and the birds in the sky and over every living creature that moves on the ground.'" (Genesis 1:27-28)

This established the principle that we are made in God's image, to live in intimate relationship with God and, through our relationship with him, we are to rule over this world as his representatives. When Adam and Eve rebelled against God they broke relationship with him and were excluded from Eden. Our position within this world, as those who were made to rule over what had been entrusted to them had not changed, but our ability to bring in God's kingdom, in partnership with him, was lost.

Fast forward to Jesus with his disciples when he says to Peter, *"I will give you the keys of the kingdom of heaven; whatever you bind on earth will be bound in heaven, and whatever you loose on earth will be loosed in heaven"* (Matthew 16: 19). He is saying, "Hey guys, I've got the keys back and I'm giving them to you. You are here to bring in the rule of God and his heavenly kingdom."

Within the New Testament there are many references to God's people being kings, ambassadors and priests. These references are not just spiritual analogies, they express physical and spiritual realities that flow from us belonging to Jesus Christ and his victory. What flows from this are incredible possibilities about our spiritual life and responsibilities as children of God. Grasping our identity and what is within us because of God's presence in us is key to understanding our significance in the kingdom. And as we take hold of this we can begin to dream and imagine what God can do through us.

Hans Christian Anderson's story of the ugly duckling is a great illustration of this. The story begins when a mother duck's eggs hatch. One of the little birds is mocked as being different and ugly, so he leaves the barnyard because he doesn't fit with the other ducks and feels rejected and hopeless. He ends up on a lake with a flock of migrating swans and risks approaching these beautiful birds. He is shocked when the swans welcome and accept him, only to realise, after looking at his reflection in the water, that he has grown into one of them. The flock takes to the air and the ugly duckling spreads his beautiful large wings and takes flight with the rest of his new family as the swan that he is.

Our enemy Satan has done a number on most of us in making us believe that we are ugly, ineffective and unable to fly as Christians. More than that, he has done a job on the whole Church, making us think that all we can do is try to remain faithful to God until we die and go to heaven. Too often in church we are simply reminded of our *sin* instead of our *significance* in the kingdom. We are no longer sinners who need forgiveness and are bound in the kingdom of darkness. We are saints – the people of God (who still struggle with sin) – who have passed from darkness into light. When we live under the shame of sin and wallow in our failures C.S. Lewis says that we are like children eating mud pies when there is a feast set at the table.

We have confused our calling with our destiny, believing that all we are called to do is wait for the day we will go to heaven. No, our *destiny* is to go to heaven, but our *calling* is to bring heaven to earth. In the Lord's prayer, Jesus taught us to pray for his kingdom in this way: *"Your kingdom come and your will be done, on earth as it is in heaven."* We have just failed to realise that he wants to use *us* to do it. In relationship with him we are to bring in his rule, and all the blessings and transforming grace that come as someone enters his kingdom.

Antoine de Saint-Exupery, a French writer and aviator who lived a life of adventure, wrote, "If you want to build a ship, don't drum up people to collect wood and don't assign them tasks and work, but rather teach them to long for the endless immensity of the sea." Before we fall into the danger of me telling you to "collect wood" with the missional tools we will look at in the second half of this book, I want to set our hearts and minds free to dream of being someone who God can use to transform others with his love and presence. I want to free us from the false image that we are "ugly ducklings", so that we can stretch our spiritual wings and soar. To do this we will look at three of the images we find in Scripture of us representing God in this world, so we grasp our significance as agents of God's kingdom.

Ambassadors:

"Therefore, if anyone is in Christ, the new creation has come: the old has gone, the new is here! All this is from God, who reconciled us to himself through Christ and gave us the ministry of reconciliation: that God was reconciling the world to himself in Christ, not counting people's sins against them. And he has committed to us the message of reconciliation. We are therefore Christ's ambassadors, as though God were making his appeal through us." (2 Corinthians 5:17-20)

This is Paul teaching the church in Corinth about the commissioning they have received from Christ. All the explanations of the role of an ambassador describe a diplomatic official of the highest rank, sent by one sovereign or state to another, as its resident representative, or an authorised messenger or representative on a temporary mission such as for negotiating a treaty. It is a rich picture of what Jesus calls his disciples to do for him – that you are a high-ranking official in the kingdom of God sent to represent Jesus and his kingdom in the mission of reconciling God's children to himself.

The job of the ambassador is to represent the sending kingdom, but also to learn the language, customs and culture of their new context. This is what Mission-Shaped Grace looks like – to be a bridge between the two kingdoms. We need to know the story and be filled with the power of the kingdom of God. But we have to learn how to express this effectively to those around us and this will require us to learn the language of our communities and understand the people around us. The second section of this book is designed to give you tools that "work" in this job of bridging between God and those around you.

The idea of being an ambassador echoes the commissioning that the risen Jesus gives to his followers as he prepares to ascend to heaven. We find this in Matthew 28 and Acts 1 and I imagine these two passages referring to different aspects of the disciples' final meeting with Jesus.

"Then Jesus came to them and said, 'All authority in heaven and on earth has been given to me. Therefore go and make disciples of all nations, baptising them in the name of the Father and of the Son and of the Holy Spirit, and teaching them to obey everything I have commanded you. And surely I am with you always, to the very end of the age.'" (Matthew 28:18-20)

"'Do not leave Jerusalem, but wait for the gift my Father promised, which you have heard me speak about. For John baptised with water, but in a few days you will be baptised with the Holy Spirit.' Then they gathered round him and asked him, 'Lord, are you at this time going to restore the kingdom to Israel?' He said to them: 'It is not for you to know the times or dates the Father has set by his own authority. But you will receive power when the Holy Spirit comes on you; and you will be my witnesses in Jerusalem, and in all Judea and Samaria, and to the ends of the earth.' After he said this, he was taken up before their very eyes, and a cloud hid him from

their sight." (Acts 1:4-9)

He commissions them to represent him and to enable others to become his followers. And what we find is that the image of being an ambassador captures the significant elements of Jesus' commission:

• Imparted power and authority
• Being a representative
• Understanding you are on mission from another kingdom

Power and authority

Jesus explains that, as he now has *all authority* he is sending his disciples in his authority. He then says, *"Wait until the Holy Spirit baptises you and you receive my power."* It must have reminded them of the time when he gave them his power and authority to go out on mission to villages, but now the commission is permanent. Authority is the position and right to exercise power, and power is the ability to move and achieve. Both are needed in order to bring transformation.

The idea that we share Christ's authority is something that many Christians seem to struggle with. Whether it feels presumptuous to claim such a position, or simply scary to believe we have the right to exercise power in Jesus' name, we find excuses to reject this idea. Yet it is vital when we think of what Jesus commissions his first disciples to do. They needed to know that they had authority over demonic spirits and sickness. This is what they were amazed by: *"even the demons submit to us in your name."* This is a perfect example of exercising Jesus' authority on his behalf. He has given us his name – the name above every name – to use as we come up against elements of the kingdom of darkness.

There is a story of a young teacher in her first year of teaching. As is often the case, she was struggling to maintain discipline in her classroom and to "own" the authority she had in her position. On one occasion she was struggling to get the class lined up in a row for their next activity. As she shouted at them once again, she was amazed to discover that this time they quickly formed a line and became quiet. She was pleased with herself, until she looked round to find the head teacher standing behind her. That is the significance of authority.

Every time we exercise authority in Jesus' name we have him standing behind us, backing up our ministry. This has been my growing experience in the healing and deliverance ministries – that where I command an evil spirit to leave, it does, and when I command sickness to be healed it increasingly is. In the physical realm I am a slightly overweight, balding, middle-aged man, but in the spiritual battle I am a knight of the kingdom who frightens the living daylights out of the kingdom of darkness! Not because of anything I have achieved, but simply because Jesus has given me his authority.

Paul explains it in Ephesians 2 with the statement, *"God raised us up with Christ and seated us in the heavenly realms in Christ Jesus"* (Ephesians 2:6). When we came to faith in Christ we were included in Jesus' resurrection and ascension. We rightly accept his death is our death, as it pays the penalty for our sin. What we often miss is that his resurrection is our resurrection and his ascension our ascension. Now that we are *"in Christ Jesus"* we can exercise his authority over this world. We are above it. We can take authority over sickness and evil in this world, because we are simultaneously ruling in the heavenly realm over them. In effect, we are *over* and not *under* our circumstances.

This is important to grasp, because in the midst of the pain and suffering of this world we can feel as though we are smaller and at the mercy of what we are facing, but actually we in authority over them. This doesn't reduce our experience of pain and suffering, and it doesn't guarantee an easy solution because Christ's reign in this realm (i.e. his kingdom) is only in part. But it transforms our perspective and creates the possibility of us bringing in the King's rule in these situations.

Authority leads to the exercise of power and Jesus told his first disciples to wait in Jerusalem for the power-giver, the Holy Spirit, to fill them. Only then will they go out as his witnesses. The order is significant. Jesus sends his Spirit into his people before he sends his people into the world. We need to follow the same order and allow the Holy Spirit to continue to fill us day by day.

My testimony is that, aged 17, I was ready to give up being a Christian. "It's too hard," I said to God, and "If you don't do something to help me then I'm going to give up." A few weeks later at a youth camp I cried out to God again and he answered my prayer and I was filled with the Holy Spirit as someone laid hands on me and spoke prophetically over my life. When I returned to school my friends wondered if I was the same person, as I couldn't stop talking about Jesus and since then I have grown in exercising his power as I have prayed and ministered to others.

My experience tells us that it is possible to be a Christian and not be filled with the power of the Holy Spirit. Paul writes, *"Be filled with the Spirit"* (Ephesians 5:18) and the original

Greek words actually mean, "Go on being filled with the Holy Spirit." If we are not filled with the Spirit we will not have the power to be the representatives Jesus calls us to be.

"Be filled with the Holy Spirit. Be filled with the Holy Spirit. Be filled with the Holy Spirit" were the simple and profound words that Ying Kai began his talk at the Exponential Conference recently. I was moved by this moment, not because I had never heard the message, but because of who was saying it. In 1995 Ying and Grace Kai were frustrated missionaries in a Chinese city. They experienced God challenge them to change their methods and to train others to be missionaries, and so they began by training one class of thirty believers. They taught the trainees that each of them had a unique story to tell of how they met Jesus. They trained them to tell their story and helped them to identify five people they would share with in the following week. In the most recent survey in 2015 of the Kais' ministry, we learn that from that group, more than 1.7 million people have come to faith and been baptised. Every month trained workers start two thousand house churches and small groups in villages, urban high-rise apartments and factories. Over 140,000 churches have been started in what is currently the world's fastest growing church planting movement.

As Ying spoke to us he was saying, "I haven't achieved this by a clever method, but by the power of the Spirit." And to have someone of such incredible fruitfulness call us back to the simplicity of, "Lord, please fill me with your Holy Spirit" was profound. We knelt on the ground and cried out for God to do that in us afresh. Some of these *Mission-Shaped Grace* practices reflect Ying's training methods, but they are empty in and of themselves without the Spirit's power.

The good news is that God has given you authority and power. When you speak and share your testimony, he accompanies it with his authority and power. When you command an illness to be healed you do it in his authority and power flows from within you to complete the kingdom work. When you speak a word of prophecy, it comes with authority and power to bring strength and freedom and open someone to God's grace. The kingdom always grows from small to large and so there is much for us to learn, and until Jesus returns his rule is not complete and so his kingdom has come and is still coming. But you and I have been given authority and power from the King of Kings.

Being a representative
The work of an ambassador is to represent the interests of the authority who sent them. As Jesus entrusts us with the ministry of reconciliation, Paul explains that he wants to make his appeal to others through us. Jesus says that, *"You will be my witnesses."* In other words, you will tell the story of who I am and what I have done. The Greek word for "witness" is *martus* from which we get the word "martyr". This is because a witness was called to stand firm and give their account of the truth, and for so many of the first Christians that meant losing their lives. It is sobering to remember that and to remember our brothers and sisters around the world who are currently representing Christ at risk of their lives, because they live in countries where Christians are persecuted. I think God is using their example to teach the Church in the West what true discipleship looks like.

And as we stand for Jesus in the places he has sent us, he is calling us to do the things he would do in those situations if he were present. It is easy for us to reduce our understanding of what being an ambassador or witness means. As we have established already, it will involve speaking for Jesus and sharing in the ministry of reconciliation; being the bridge that reconnects the people around us with God.

But we cannot represent a supernatural God without being willing to do the supernatural things of his kingdom. Somehow our pattern of mission has often been completely devoid of any demonstration of the kingdom. The whole missional strategy of Acts could be summarised as: get filled with the Holy Spirit, proclaim the Gospel, do supernatural things that get people's attention, explain that it is Jesus who is doing these things. When we get an understanding that we are to be Christ to those around us, we will begin to understand that we should do what Jesus would do: heal the sick, release the Holy Spirit's power, show radical love and compassion, etc.

Often it has been in the moments when the last thing I wanted to do was to offer to pray for someone, but I have been obedient to the Holy Spirit's promptings, that God has done the most amazing things. I think he is trying to teach me that the authority and power come from Jesus and he is just looking for someone to do what he wants to do in a person's life, and he will use anyone who is available.

I remember when I was leading a youth group and we were playing rounders at a local park. A teenage girl was sitting under a tree and not joining in. When I asked her why, she explained that she had damaged her sciatic nerve during the week and she was taking strong painkillers that made her dozy and she was still in a great deal of pain. As we carried on with the games I couldn't shake off the nagging thought that I should pray for her. But I really didn't want to. I was tired, it felt risky, and I had no faith that it would actually work.

So I did a deal with God that if she came back to the church afterwards, and if there was a moment when I could talk to her alone, that I would pray with her (along with one of the female leaders). Of course, all of those things happened and when we prayed with her she was immediately healed and literally did cartwheel after cartwheel around the church car park!

Understanding you are on a mission from another kingdom
After Jesus rose from the dead, Luke records that he spent 40 days revealing himself to his followers and teaching them about the kingdom (Acts 1). This was Jesus' central message, that he was bringing in the rule of God on this earth. And in the Matthew and Acts passages Jesus talks about "all nations" and being witnesses "to the ends of the earth". His kingdom is to expand and touch the whole world and every different nation and he will need people to bring in his kingdom in these different places. It might be helpful to think of yourself as, "Christ's ambassador to ..." and insert the name of your school, your family or your workplace. Now that you have your job title and mission, what could you do to represent Jesus to them?

To conclude this section: we have simply established that from Paul's imagery of an ambassador, which summarises Jesus' commissioning of his first disciples, we are called to represent Jesus to those around us. The question that flows from this is, *do you believe that you are Christ's ambassador? That he has given you power and authority as he did his first disciples so that you can heal the sick and demonstrate the kingdom is here? That you are his representative, sent to lead others into relationship with him?*

The answers to these questions really matter.

Sons (and daughters!)

Before I offend everyone about the lack of gender equality in the section title, I want to take some time to explain that the concept of "sonship" in the New Testament applies to male and female Christians. There are five verses in which the Greek word *huiothesia*, translated "sonship" or "adoption to sons" occurs: Romans 8:15, 23, 9:4; Galatians 4:5; and Ephesians 1:5. This literally means to "set someone as a son". It is a legal term borrowed by Paul from the Roman court system of his day.

In the Roman world of the first century, an adopted son was a son deliberately chosen by his adoptive father to continue his name and inherit his estate. Often these boys would be slaves and be adopted by wealthy parents who had no sons. The boy was adopted through a legal process in which he had his debts cancelled, received full status as a son, the rights to his share of his father's property, and was in no way inferior in status to a son born naturally. In fact, he had a protected legal status in which the father was now unable to disinherit him. The father gave up the right ever to do this. So this word for "sonship" conveys a number of vital truths that we must not lose – the idea of full status, equal inheritance and permanency. It is for this reason that we will continue to use it with the understanding that it applies spiritually to male and female, and so in effect means "sons and daughters".

Many others have written in greater depth about the personal significance of discovering the truth that we are no longer orphans and slaves, but are children of God, and how this brings emotional healing and freedom. But I have a concern that the recovery of the understanding of the "Father-heart of God" can end up in sentimentalism and self-who do you think you are?

comfort and it misses the fullness of all that it means to be God's child.

In our current culture the therapeutic benefits of the Gospel are often presented without the cost of the call to follow Jesus. The purpose of this section is to persuade you that you hold the position of a son of God. What flows from this truth is that you are to do and be like your heavenly Father. We are meant to be a "chip off the old block", "like Father like son" and to carry his image in all we do.

This idea of sons growing up to be like their fathers was the norm of Jesus' day. In that culture it was assumed that a son would train under his father and eventually enter into the same trade. When Jesus says, *"Blessed are the peacemakers, for they shall be called sons of God"* (Matthew 5:9) he is saying that God is a peacemaker, and so when we work for peace we are acting like sons of God because we are like God in this respect. Like Father, like son.

This is seen most clearly in John 5 when Jesus is accused of blasphemy because of his response to the Pharisees' complaints about his Sabbath healing. Jesus answered simply, *"My Father is working until now, and I am working"* (John 5:17). The implication of Jesus' reply is, "God is my father, and I am his son and as he is always at work healing, even on the Sabbath, it is right that as his son I should be healing on the Sabbath, because sons are supposed to do what their Fathers do."

The very next verse tells us that the Pharisees understood this: *"This was why the Jews were seeking all the more to kill him, because not only was he breaking the Sabbath, but he was even calling God his own Father, making himself equal with God."*

97

When Jesus indicated that he was doing the work of his Father, it was an implicit claim to equality with the Father, that he was a full inheritor of everything that is his Father's. The Jews were angry because they understood the deeper meaning of Jesus' words. It would have been blasphemy had it not been true.

We cannot claim to be sons of God in the same way as Jesus is: the eternal not created, fully human–fully God, perfect Son of God. But this does not deny the significance of us being God's child. This is why Paul borrows the concept of sonship. We have to be saved and rescued and adopted from our slavery to sin, to become sons of God. But we have been made God's sons and daughters and so we must not reduce our status, our full inheritance, and the expectation that we will be able to do what our heavenly Father does.

In other words, we heal the sick because our Father is God and he heals the sick. We can do this because of our identity as sons, not because we are performing a task. When we act like God we are living out of our identity. Only God can do miracles and our *Abba*, our "Dad", is in charge of the universe. When we realise we are sons and daughters of the King of the Universe, and we have received a full inheritance won for us by our brother, Jesus, we will start to act like it. Like Father, like son; a chip off the old block. Kris Vallotton said, "It's when you realise who you are that you realise you have been behaving below your nature and that you were living short of your potential."

Priests

"You also, like living stones, are being built into a spiritual house to be a holy priesthood, offering spiritual sacrifices

acceptable to God through Jesus Christ ... you are a chosen people, a royal priesthood, a holy nation, God's special possession, that you may declare the praises of him who called you out of darkness into his wonderful light." (1 Peter 2:5, 9)

The Catholic, Orthodox and Anglican denominations have hijacked the word "priest" to be the title of their church ministers. Yet it is a distortion of the term and has led to a tradition that undermines the principle Peter is teaching here. The New Testament is clear that we are *all* priests.

To try and communicate this one day I decided to ordain the whole of our Sunday evening congregation. I led about 150 people through the Anglican ordination prayers and responses, and then at the end I gave them all cardboard dog collars and they all clipped them around their necks. It might sound ridiculous (and it was a pretty strange sight!), but I was trying to break down the idea of the "clergy–laity" divide. To underline the truth that each person was as much a priest as I am. In the Church in recent years there have been many developments in lay ministry to ensure that churches stop being one-man-bands and become the body of Christ, with everyone playing their part. The problem is that this movement often feels like clergy graciously allowing lay people to take certain roles. Instead, what I believe God is wanting to communicate is that *every role* is open to *everyone,* because we are all priests and we all have the authority to exercise priestly ministry.

Of course, God gives specific anointing, grace and authority to church leaders to exercise their calling. But the church leader's role is not to do all the ministry and let members of the church help with those things he hasn't got enough time to do (or doesn't want to!) Instead, Paul's understanding of the church leaders' roles was to equip the people of God for their ministry, so that each person was able to fulfil their role (Ephesians 4:12-16).

Kierkegaard explained it in this way: he likened the church to the theatre, in which there is a single or small group of actors, a prompt to remind them of the script, and an audience watching the performance. He said that the church is organised as if the church leader is the actor, the Holy Spirit is the prompt, and the congregation is the audience. But God's view of the church is that the congregation are the actors, the church leader (under the guidance of the Spirit) is the prompt, and God is the audience. We are all priests.

The reason why the concept of priesthood is important is because it communicates what our role in this world is – and that is to connect heaven and earth. It is the biblical basis for the idea of us being a bridge that connects people with God. God's version of a priest is not someone in a church leadership position, but someone who bears his image and represents him on earth. When Peter declares that the church is a *"royal priesthood, a holy nation"* he is building on the declarations made to the people of Israel.

In Exodus God tells Moses to say to the people, *"You will be for me a kingdom of priests and a holy nation. These are the words you are to speak to the Israelites"* (Exodus 19:6). If you know your Old Testament then you will know that the tribe of Levi were the focus of priesthood within Israel and fulfilled the necessary duties around the tabernacle and temple. But the identity of the whole nation of Israel was that they were to be God's priests, his representatives on earth, in that they maintained his presence on earth, declared the truth about who God is, and were the source through which God would bless every nation on the earth as he prophesied to Abram (Genesis 12:3).

The Levitical priest's role can be summarised as: carrying God's presence, bringing the people to God through the presentation of sacrifices on their behalf, and bringing God to the people as they declared his blessing over them (Deuteronomy 10:8). In Numbers 6 God gives Moses clear instructions:

"The Lord said to Moses, 'Tell Aaron and his sons, "This is how you are to bless the Israelites. Say to them, 'The Lord bless you and keep you; the Lord make his face shine on you and be gracious to you; the Lord turn his face towards you and give you peace.'" So they will put my name on the Israelites, and I will bless them.'" (Numbers 6:22-27)

When Peter then applies the concept of being priests to followers of Jesus we need to understand what this means. Often in Scripture, the New Testament explains that God gave an example of something in his instructions to Israel. This contained the principles he now wants to work out fully through the Church, empowered by the Holy Spirit. So there is a "type" of priest in the Levitical priesthood, the principles of which now need to be applied to the Church and fulfilled completely – now that God has given his Spirit to all his people. The problem has been that we applied the model to church leaders and not to all Christians.

As always, the move from the Old to the New Testament covenants involves an expansion of grace and power. So now we do not simply maintain God's presence at the heart of the temple, like a Levitical priest, rather *we are the temples* of the Holy Spirit (1 Corinthians 6:19, 2 Corinthians 6:16).

And now we all have the authority to bring the blessing of God from heaven to earth. This should change how we pray. Too often our prayers our timid, with sub-clauses inserted in case what we are praying is not the will of God. One type of prayer which needs to be restored to our tool kit is the prayer of authority, in which we declare over people the blessing and purposes of God. This will only happen if we understand that we have been authorised as priests to act on behalf of the King and that we can pray from the throne where we are seated with Christ, as well as to the throne from earth.

Bill Johnson illustrates it in this way: at work, if you were told to do something by your boss, and you kept going back to him again and again, asking him to do it instead of you, then you would eventually get sacked. Jesus commissioned us to heal the sick, drive out evil spirits, and proclaim that the kingdom of heaven has come on earth, and we keep asking him to heal the sick, etc. The model Jesus gave us, and the one the first apostles demonstrated, was one in which *they* commanded blessing and healing. In Ephesians we are taught to pray with *"all kinds of prayers and requests"* (Ephesians 6:18). So we have to learn when our priestly role involves declaring blessing from heaven to earth, and when it involves bringing people and situations to God and asking for his help. My guess is that most of us need to grasp more of the authority we have as priests, which allows us to bless and declare things in Jesus' name.

If you need an example of how this is not just a form of words, but a form of prayer that releases the power and presence of God, I can't think of a better one than from our additional needs Sunday-School group. There is one child in this group with autism and limited speech, who comes in and bounces energetically around the room. The team's difficulty is how to enable him to connect with God through the stories and songs. A clear highlight of the morning is when the team prays blessing over him with a simple white sheet lifted gently lift up and down above him. He gradually settles into a lying position under the sheet and relaxes. Those holding the corners of the sheet continue to pray blessings, speak God's love over him, or pray silently, or with tongues. Each time it finishes he gets up with a beaming smile and hugs the team. No words, but so much communication. One child with Downs Syndrome often asks for the prayer time because she seems to find it an emotional release and sometimes weeps. She says that she loves Jesus.

PRESS PAUSE

As we finish this chapter I encourage you to thank God for who he has made you to be in Christ. Thanksgiving is the route into many things in God's kingdom. The Psalmist says that we should enter God's presence with thanksgiving in our hearts (Psalm 100:4). Paul explains the way to have peace as we pray is to ask with thanksgiving (Philippians 4:6) and the way to enter into our identity in Christ is to thank God for the truth of all we have just read. It is the best weapon against the lies of the enemy as we accept what God has said to be true about us. Thanksgiving takes God at his word and allows the Spirit to speak that truth to our spirits (Romans 8:16) so that we rise up into our true identity. So take the truths of this chapter and thank God that they are true for you and see how the Spirit then wants to reveal more of all that God has for you.

"One type of prayer which
needs to be restored to our tool
kit is the prayer of authority, in
which we declare over people
the blessing and purposes of
God. This will only happen if we
understand that we have been
authorised as priests to act on
behalf of the King..."

Chapter 5
Conclusion

I hope that by now I have convinced you that when you came to faith in Jesus Christ he renewed you, changed your identity, and called you into his kingdom mission. And that Jesus has left us, in his word, clear patterns and principles of how we can be those disciple-making disciples. This call to join in with the mission of God is an invitation to adventure and is not without cost and risk.

In 1980 a young man from Rwanda was forced by his tribe to either renounce Christ or face certain death. He refused to renounce Christ and he was killed on the spot. The night before he had written the following commitment which was found in his room:

"I'm part of the fellowship of the unashamed, the die has been cast, I have stepped over the line, the decision has been made – I'm a disciple of Jesus Christ. I won't look back, let up, slow down, back away or be still. My past is redeemed, my present makes sense, my future is secure. I'm finished and done with low living, sight walking, smooth knees, colourless dreams, tamed vision, worldly talking, cheap giving and dwarfed goals. My face is set, my gait is fast, my goal is heaven, my road is narrow, my way is rough, my companions are few, my guide is reliable, my mission is clear. I won't give up, shut up, let up until I have stayed up, stored up, and prayed up for the cause of Jesus Christ. I must go till He comes, give till I drop, preach till everyone knows, work till He stops me and when He comes for His own, He will have no trouble recognising me because my banner will have been clear."

This statement reflects someone who has grasped the significance of living as a follower of Jesus. In the UK, following Jesus is unlikely to cost you your life, but the same attitude should characterise our faith. Mission is not meant to be an addition to our current way of life, it is meant to transform every part of it, so that our identity as Jesus-followers becomes our primary identity.

Jesus spoke very clearly about the need to die to ourselves in order to find life in him: *"Whoever wants to be my disciple must deny themselves and take up their cross and follow me. For whoever wants to save their life will lose it, but whoever loses their life for me and for the gospel will save it"* (Mark 8:35-38)

There was only one place someone was going if they were carrying a cross – to die. It is the equivalent of the walk of a death-row prisoner from their cell to be executed. In US prisons, as they did this guards used to announce, "Dead man walking! Dead man walking here!" That is what we are to be as Christians: living sacrifices in which we are living our lives, but dead to our own ambitions and agendas. The trouble is, as we think about the call to be involved in God's kingdom mission, we so easily seek to hold on to our lives, our reputations, our comforts and our priorities. So when Jesus calls us to speak for him we aren't available. Dietrich Bonhoeffer captured the challenge of denying ourselves when he wrote, "When Christ calls a man, he bids him come and die."

A couple of years ago, Andrew White, the "vicar of Bagdad" spoke at Holy Trinity Church – a truly humbling experience hearing about his life of service and sacrifice in staying in a city where his life was constantly in danger because he longed to share the Gospel with people there. His parting encouragement at the end of his sermon was that instead of saying "take care" to another Christian when we say goodbye to them, we should say "take risks". Take risks for God. We will only do this if the whole of our life is entrusted to him.

As we finish this section, and before we begin to work practically on the missional practices, I encourage you to take some time to rededicate yourself to Jesus as his devoted disciple. The willingness to take risks comes from a decision to trust the whole of our lives to God. This dedication flows from knowing his love and goodness and from a desire to glorify him in response to him being God and having saved us.

Methodists hold an annual Covenant Service, at which they celebrate all that God has done and rededicate themselves to God using a Covenant Prayer. The words of the Methodist Covenant Prayer are shown below and are serious and not light and easy to say. Take some time to read them over and allow the whole-life encompassing nature of them draw you to a place where you give yourself afresh to God.

I am no longer my own but yours.
Put me to what you will, rank me with whom you will;
put me to doing,
put me to suffering;
let me be employed for you,

or laid aside for you,
exalted for you,
or brought low for you;
let me be full,
let me be empty,
let me have all things,
let me have nothing:
I freely and wholeheartedly yield all things
to your pleasure and disposal.
And now, glorious and blessed God,
Father, Son and Holy Spirit,
you are mine and I am yours. So be it.
And the covenant now made on earth, let it be ratified in heaven.

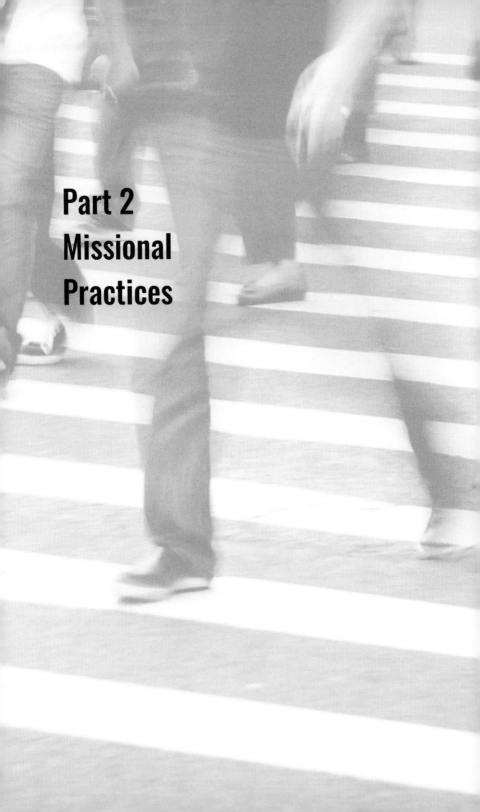

Part 2
Missional
Practices

Generosity

 Receiving and
Releasing

 Asking Questions
and Telling Stories

 Calling

 Eating Together

Introduction

The Israelites were having one of their many spats with the Philistines during King Saul's reign, recorded in 1 Samuel 13. Then they hit a problem: they didn't have enough weapons. We read that,

"Not a blacksmith could be found in the whole land of Israel, because the Philistines had said, 'Otherwise the Hebrews will make swords or spears!'" (1 Samuel 13:19)

This was the enemy's strategy, to remove the people who made and sharpened swords so the Israelites were literally blunted. It feels as if that has been the enemy's strategy against the Church. Our mission has been blunted and those who know how to confidently produce disciples who will reach others, heal the sick and proclaim the Gospel of the kingdom are few and far between. The aim of these five missional practices is to put some weapons in your hands or to sharpen what you are already doing.

A few years ago, we surveyed our missional community leadership teams and asked everyone, "How many of you have shared your faith, told your story, or offered to pray with someone who is not yet a Christian within the last year?" The response was less than 20%. These were the leaders of our missional communities – the stars of our show, the mature Christians! It confirmed how that, despite the vision and strategy we had implemented to create missional communities, individually we were still lacking confidence in how to make disciples. We then started to be intentional about training people in the tools contained in this section. A year later we asked people the same question and over 80% had now done something, shared something, sought to reach out to someone. Applying these five missional practices will enable you to do the same.

Before you start to look at each of these practices I want to get something straight: *you are incompetent!* I'm genuinely not wanting to be rude, but to make sure that you acknowledge your need to learn. As Claude Bernard, a French scientist, said, "It's what we think we know that keeps us from learning." If you are currently living the full life of a disciple who makes other disciples, who then go on to do the same, then you don't need to keep reading. But if you're like most Christians in the West, I'm guessing that you haven't been significantly involved in making many disciple-making disciples. We all have much to learn.

So we have some work to do and I encourage you to join me in acknowledging our incompetence. Why? Because in stopping the pretence that we are living the full life of a disciple we open the door to growth and change. The Four Stages of Competence is a model that describes the process of learning a new skill.

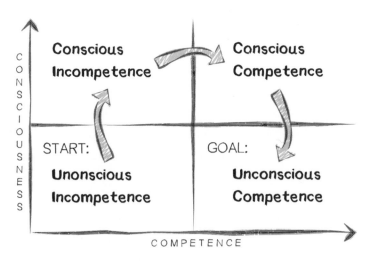

The Four Stages of Competence

It shows that at the start we are often oblivious to the depths of our incompetence, we're just excited to be having a go. But as we start the process of learning, we soon discover how much harder it is than it looks. We become aware of our limitations and as we become conscious of our incompetence we can become discouraged by our lack of progress and poor ability. This is a risky moment when we are tempted to give up, but we are actually making real progress, because we now know what we need to learn. If we persevere we will progress and become conscious of our growing competence. Eventually we will be able to do what we want to do without even thinking of the process needed to achieve it – *unconscious competence*.

Jesus did this with his disciples. When he called them to follow him they excitedly left their nets and followed him, no doubt with dreams of what it would be like to follow him. But there were moments of real failure and discouragement when instead of the kingdom growing, people started to leave, or they failed to cast out a demon, or cowered in fear at the storm, and they were tempted to give up. They realised how much they still had to learn.

I share all of this because developing the lifestyle of a missional disciple is not easy. You will have moments where it isn't working and real disappointments. But don't give up. This is just the process of learning. I am confident that if you persevere in this you will lead someone else to put their trust in Jesus and receive his gift of eternal life. How can I be so sure? Five reasons:

- You do not have a defective version of the Holy Spirit within you and he has been sent to be your helper and to empower you as a witness of Jesus.
- The Gospel really does work.-It is the power of God to save.
- Jesus is determined to build his Church and extend his kingdom and when anyone steps forward in mission you can be sure he will use them.
- The love of God for lost people means that he is already at work in people and looking for someone to lead them back to him.
- I have seen again and again that when people are willing to learn these practices, other people come to faith.

Having laid the foundations we are now going to get really practical and put some tools in your hands. This section looks at the five G.R.A.C.E missional practices – the bridge building tools that will allow the grace of God to flow from you to those around you. As you engage with these practices have trust that God is with you by his Spirit. Be willing to persevere and to keep practising. Go for it!

1
Generosity:
looking for opportunities to bless others

Introduction

Imagine the difference the church could make in the community if we were known as the most generous and compassionate people. No-strings-attached generosity was the hallmark of the first century Church. It should be a hallmark of the 21st Century Church too.

We don't use the word "grace" very much in our everyday lives, but if there is a word in our current language that connects most closely with the idea of grace, I think it is *generosity*. The idea of grace is God showing us undeserved favour and blessing us. In God's two big actions, creation and salvation, we see his generosity. What an amazing world God has created for us. He has blessed us with unnecessary riches beyond what is required for sustaining life: billions of stars, thousands of species, the care with which he has designed us and "knitted us together", the way in which we experience life through our senses in colour and sound and touch. All of these things are beyond the bare necessities of life. They reveal God's extravagant generosity; his desire for us to be blessed and have a tangible experience of his goodness.

And when it comes to salvation we read the most famous

verse in the Bible: *"God so loved the world that he gave his only Son"* (John 3:16). Out of God's love for us he gave the most precious gift he could in order to save us. His love caused him to be generous and to give. He demonstrates giving and not counting the cost. Giving without strings attached. As someone has said, "You can give without loving, but you can't love without giving."

There is a great story of Alexander the Great who was passing a beggar by the roadside. The beggar called out for alms and Alexander threw him some gold coins. One of his servants was shocked and said, "Sire, copper coins would have adequately met the beggar's needs. Why give him gold coins?" Alexander replied, "Copper coins would have met the beggar's needs, but gold coins suit Alexander's giving."

God's generosity reveals his love and grace towards us, and our generosity needs to reflect his.

God is calling you and me to represent him to the world around us. Too often the Church has been mean-spirited and tight-fisted and people have got the impression from us that God is like that too. Nothing could be further from the truth! So if we are to paint an accurate picture of God in this world and allow his love to flow through us to others, we will need to reflect his generosity.

Principle

When God called Abram and promised to make his descendants a great nation, God explained his purpose to Abram: *"I will make you into a great nation, and I will bless you ... and all peoples on earth will be blessed through you"* (Genesis 12:2-3). So God's people were blessed in order to be a blessing – and yet they constantly forgot it.

Jesus lived a life of generosity as he loved and blessed people who had no chance of ever paying him back. He honoured outcasts, women, children – the nobodies of his society. He gave himself for others. And the Jewish leaders became angrier and angrier the more he did it – a sobering reminder that the ones who were the experts in God's law were the ones who completely failed to recognise the fulfilment of that word in Jesus.

When Jesus wanted to teach people to do the same he told the parable of the good Samaritan: we are to be generous, even to those we would call our enemies. If we didn't get it from the parable, he then he spelled it out for us:

"Love your enemies, do good to those who hate you, bless those who curse you, pray for those who mistreat you." (Luke 6:27-28)

This is *Mission-Shaped Grace* – the early Church got it. They were famous for the way they blessed others and cared for the poor in their community (Acts 2:44-45).

The apostle Paul told Timothy,

"Command those who are rich in this present world not to be arrogant nor to put their hope in wealth, which is so uncertain, but to put their hope in God, who richly provides us with everything for our enjoyment. Command them to do good, to be rich in good deeds, and to be generous and willing to share. In this way they will lay up treasure for themselves as a firm foundation for the coming age, so that they may take hold of the life that is truly life." (1 Timothy 6:17-19)

Three principles are important here that release generosity:

1. Our generosity is a response to God's generosity to us. Freely we have received, freely we give. Everything we have is from God who richly provides and allows us to enjoy his provision. But it is not ours to hold on to. The call to be generous is simply the call to use what he has given to us.

I sometimes use an illustration with children to show this. I take ten £1 coins and give them to a child, then just as they are about to walk away I say, "Would you mind giving me one of those back as I need it for something else." When they have done that I say, "Would you mind giving one to that person over there and one to that person over there?" Then we have a conversation about how they now have £7 that they didn't have before. I ask how they feel about that and they invariably say, "Very happy." Then I ask how it felt to have given £1 back to me and £2 to others – and they are fine with that. In two minutes we have established the joy of tithing 10% to God and giving to others on top of this.

2. It is God's love and goodness that sets us free to be generous. God cares for us and the blessing we receive frees us to bless others. This is vital to understand because if we are not confident in his love and care for us we will self-protect and live with the fear that in the future we may lack something or miss out on something if we focus our attention on blessing others. The Lord is our good shepherd, therefore we lack nothing.

3. Generosity requires us to have a true value of things. If our hearts are set on comfort and consumption we will not be free to be generous to others with our time or money. Selfishness and fear rob us of the ability to be generous. I heard of a pastor from a country where Christians are persecuted explaining to a US pastor about why he had seen thousands of people converted and the American hadn't. He simply said, "You teach people to look for rewards in this life, we teach eternal rewards." In other words, the reason that his people were dynamically reaching out to others and sacrificing and serving in order to see others come to Christ, was because they weren't focused on making themselves comfortable. As disciples of Jesus we cannot live life like a self-fulfilment programme, as our society tells us to. Instead we have to live as citizens of heaven, longing for home, storing up treasure there and living with a freedom to risk our comfort in order to bless others and tell them about Jesus.

Presence

The reason why simple acts of generosity can be so powerful is because they line up with God's heart and allow his love to touch a person's life. We were created to be blessed and when someone is generous to us I think it cuts through our rational thoughts and touches something inside us. Steve Sjogren, who wrote about "servant evangelism" – sharing the Good News through blessing others – says, "Small acts of kindness, done with great love, can change the world."

It's as if when we love someone and express it through practical generosity, it builds a connection with them and opens them up for God's love to come in. I don't think the human heart or soul can resist no-strings generosity. And when we start to ask Jesus, "Who do you want me to bless this week?" we give him a chance to show us who he is already at work in, or where he is wanting to care for someone, and we get to be his blessing to another human being – how cool is that?! We are agents of the kingdom of heaven and we are to express here on earth the generosity that exists in God's heart and heavenly kingdom. When we do that we can be sure God is going to be present and wants to join in with what we're doing.

I remember once when I was in the supermarket buying milk and cookies for a church meeting. I was already late (as always!) and the woman in front of me was taking ages to pay. She then said to the cashier, "I haven't got enough money, I'll have to take some things off." I was very annoyed and thought some uncharitable things about her. But then a small voice inside me said, "You pay for it." As I realised this was the Holy Spirit prompting me, I offered to pay and she accepted. I thought that she would be grateful and God would touch her through this, but she hurried off with hardly a thank you. But then the woman at the checkout asked me why I was buying so much milk and I told her it was for church. "Oh," she said, "that's why you were kind and paid for that lady's shopping." I asked her about any faith she had and then asked if I could pray for her for anything, which she let me do at the checkout. A small act of generosity opened her up to the grace of God.

Practice

So this missional practice is all about asking God to give us the opportunity to be generous to others and bless them. Generosity is anything that is done out of a desire to love and bless another person, carried out in such a way that we don't count the cost. In other words, we don't expect to be repaid. There are no strings attached and we don't hold it over them. One way of getting a sense of call and focus on this is to think of the places where God has put you, and the people he has surrounded you with.

Mapping Your Relational World

Take some time to get a clear picture of the people who you see regularly in your daily life and with whom you have some kind of relationship. You can then "map" your relationship with them and with each other. See the diagram below.

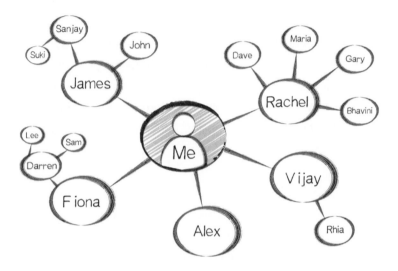

Mapping your relational world

Draw a circle at the centre of a page. Write your name in that centre circle. Now draw circles around it. Write the names of the people you know and love who are far from God. Use the circles around their names to add people they know and who you share a relationship with, such as children or partners of people you know. You now have the names of people you can pray for to come to faith in Jesus. Think about which five people you feel the strongest burden to pray for their salvation. Make a list of their names or pray for these people for at least 5 minutes every day. You might find it helpful to put this list somewhere you see every day e.g. in the book/

Bible you're reading, as the background on your phone, or on your bathroom mirror!

Pray daily for them and seek opportunities to bless and share with them. Here is an example of how to pray blessings on people:

"James, I bless you in the name of the Lord Jesus. May you know the Lord's protection and peace today. I bless you with the desire to know God and the freedom to begin to seek after him. I bless you with a revelation of God's love for you. May his presence touch you. May a word in a song or film cause to you to think about him. May you know him speaking to you in your dreams. James, may God bless you today in Jesus' name."

Blessing Others

As we consider blessing others we need to be creative in how we think about this. It might be that you are able to serve someone and meet their need. Or it might simply be something that is a small act of kindness, done to bless someone and brighten their day. As Mother Theresa said, "We shall never know all the good that a simple smile can do."

Here are some practical ways to be generous:

Practically:

Buying a small gift, baking a cake, lending someone a tool that they need, offering to babysit, giving them a lift, or helping with decorating a room. This may not seem the most radical evangelistic plan, but simple acts can really touch someone's heart. We have a temptation to protect our property and live independent lives, so when we live differently we help to show people the difference God's love makes in our lives.

Words:
Look for opportunities to speak words of blessing and encouragement over others. Try to make it a practice to say thank you to others and say what you appreciate about them. Publicly honour someone in front of others in order to build their self-esteem and reputation. Write a card to someone to say how much they mean to you. At work promote someone else's success instead of your own.

Time:
In our stressed and stretched lives one of the most generous acts can be to give time to someone. A willingness to be interrupted and allow our schedule to change in order to help someone is an expression of generosity. It could be to stop and help carry a heavy suitcase up some stairs, give someone a lift in your car when it is out of your way, or stay late after an event to help clear up, or simply listen to someone. Time is precious and people are blessed when we give them time.

Financially:
It could be as simple as buying someone a coffee, or it might be that God calls you to meet a significant financial need for someone. We have to be careful to be generous financially in a way that the other person knows they are not obliged to us and we are not making them our debtor. But equally we musn't be too "English" about money and refuse to get involved and support someone because it feels too awkward.

Spiritually:
As you meet with people, silently pray blessings on them while you with them. This works for everyone you meet –

even your difficult colleague! A key way to have your heart changed towards someone who you find difficult, or who has hurt you, is to choose to forgive them and then start to regularly pray blessing on them. This is generosity in its clearest form. We have to do as Jesus taught us: not just to pray for our enemies, but actually do good to them. *"Bless those who curse you"* (Luke 6:28)

Hospitality:

This is a high value in the New Testament: simply inviting someone into our home, making them welcome, honouring them by serving them. When was the last time you invited someone into your home?

PRESS PLAY

Time to stop reading and actually do something. Don't move on from this chapter without putting a plan together about how you are going to build a pattern of blessing others regularly. Remember, you are trying to develop a missional lifestyle of repeatable patterns that will keep you involved in God's mission for the rest of your life – not just a one-off action to tick a box.

First of all, map out the people with whom you are regularly in relationship who don't know Jesus. Then write the names of the five people you are going to pray for daily on a piece of paper and place it somewhere it will catch your attention every day. Here is a suggestion of what to do at the beginning of each day:

Take time to thank God for his blessings, remembering his care for you. Then ask him, "Lord, who do you want me to bless today?" Wait to see if a name or situation or need comes to mind. If not, simply go into that day on the lookout for opportunities to bless others.

Pray blessings on those five people and ask God to draw them closer to him.

Individual or Group Study

IN
How are you?
Is there something you are thankful for?
When has someone been generous to you and what difference did it make to you?
How are you doing in living generously towards others?

UP
Read John 2:1-11
What does this teach us about God?
(Look at what Jesus reveals to us about God when he turns water into wine and blesses this couple's wedding)
What does this teach us about people?
(Look at Jesus' example of blessing others, Mary's example of faith, and the role of the servants in enabling the miracle to take place)
How do you need to respond?

OUT
Take your plan of action and pray over it for God to guide you in being a blessing to others. Make specific plans about how you can bless someone this week and offer it to God.

"The reason why simple acts of
generosity can be so powerful is because
they line up with God's heart and allow
his love to touch a person's life."

2
Receiving and Releasing God's Presence: learning to recognise and respond to the presence of God in each situation

Introduction

Wouldn't it be amazing if we experienced God speaking to us and present with us in our workplace or in the restaurant or in the stands of the football stadium?! The Gospels and the book of Acts are the story of God's kingdom coming in everyday lives and situations. There were no church services or buildings to describe back then.

Jesus healed the sick at the swimming pool, the picnic site, the roadside and in people's homes. As Christians we are meant to be streams of God's grace, not stagnant pools or dried-up river beds. If that is to be the case, then we have to develop two practices: a willingness to receive God's presence and a desire to give it away.

It seems obvious, and yet Christians who love to receive from God often seem unwilling to get off their backsides and do something with it. This is why the Charismatic movement has sometimes ended up in cul-de-sacs, or people have become disillusioned with it. The gifts of the Spirit were never meant to be confined to a church service, they were given to empower and equip the church for mission. And those who are practical, with a desire to serve, can easily do so in their own strength and can't see the need for all that "spiritual stuff" in which the Holy Spirit refreshes and renews us. This is the opposite danger, in which the church becomes an extension of social services by simply organising provision for people's needs. Without a willingness to bring God's presence into a situation where we are serving, it is easy for it to simply be *us* that people get to know instead of *Jesus*. This is why grace and mission have to come together – one without the other is lacking something. Grace becomes stale and stagnant when it isn't expressed in mission. Mission is powerless and mechanical without the empowering presence of God's grace. So let's learn how to receive and release God's presence wherever we are.

Principle

"Jesus said, 'Let anyone who is thirsty come to me and drink. Whoever believes in me, as Scripture has said, rivers of living water will flow from within them.' By this he meant the Spirit, whom those who believed in him were later to receive." (John 7:37-39)

Here we clearly see this principle of receiving and releasing God's presence. We first have to receive the Holy Spirit, admitting our spiritual thirst and need. Then, as we have received him, we then allow him to flow from within us into others' lives. In other words, *the Holy Spirit is in you and he wants out!* The amazing thing Jesus teaches is that from our "drinking" of the Spirit he will become a river flowing out of us.

Jesus is actually teaching us about what he experienced himself – he lived for 30 years before he started his ministry of bringing in God's kingdom. And Luke records that it is as the Holy Spirit fills him at his baptism (Luke 3:22), and then empowers him as he comes out of the wilderness (Luke 4:14), that he begins his ministry. He then stands up in the synagogue and deliberately reads from the prophet Isaiah:

"'The Spirit of the Lord is on me, because he has anointed me to proclaim good news to the poor. He has sent me to proclaim freedom for the prisoners and recovery of sight for the blind, to set the oppressed free, to proclaim the year of the Lord's favour.' Then he rolled up the scroll, gave it back to the attendant and sat down. The eyes of everyone in the synagogue were fastened on him. He began by saying to them, 'Today this scripture is fulfilled in your hearing.'" (Luke 4:18-19)

Jesus shows us what it is to receive the Holy Spirit, then that he understood the reason for the Spirit's anointing was to go and set the captives free – which he did as he healed the sick and cast out demons, proclaiming God's good news and loving people with compassion. This is Jesus-shaped ministry. As his body on earth, the Church should look like him.

In case we think it was only Jesus who could do this, he commissions the twelve disciples to do the same:

"As you go, proclaim this message: 'The kingdom of heaven has come near.' Heal the sick, raise the dead, cleanse those who have leprosy, drive out demons. Freely you have received; freely give." (Matthew 10:7-8)

Jesus explains the dynamics of kingdom living as *receiving* and *releasing*. You have received freely, now go and give it away freely. This pattern of receiving and releasing is the key to living like Jesus.

Presence

A big battle for us is to recognise that God is constantly present in us and with us. We have to live with an awareness of the presence of God with us wherever we are. We will look at how to do this in the practical section in a moment, but the key is to recognise that wherever we are, God is present with us. *What difference does that make?* The potential and possibilities that result from God being present in any situation are incredible. As Paul teaches, *"If the Spirit of him who raised Jesus from the dead is living in you, he who raised Christ from the dead will also give life to your mortal bodies because of his Spirit who lives in you"* (Romans 8:11). Paul is teaching us to realise what has changed because the Holy Spirit is in us. We have all of the power of God with us in any moment.

Peter realised this when he was going to the temple with John (Acts 3). A lame man asked him for money. Peter says, *"Silver and gold I don't have, but what I do have I give you. In the name of Jesus Christ of Nazareth, get up and walk."* Peter recognised that he had the presence of God in him and that he also had the authority to release his presence and bring healing. Do you realise that all of this is true for you as well? We have to have something to give, or rather *someone* to give – the person of the Holy Spirit. You can only give away something that you know you have.

Practice

Receiving God's presence:

As we have established already, it is vital that we are filled with the Spirit. It is possible to live a life without being full of the Spirit, so we need to pray for this. I'm not talking about a one-off experience that keeps us topped up for the rest of our lives. My experience has been that I pray daily for the Spirit to fill me, but I also need regular times in which I open myself to God and allow someone else to pray for me to be filled with the Holy Spirit. I'm amazed at the number of Christians who have never had someone lay hands on them and pray for the Holy Spirit to fill them. The reason I am amazed is because it happened again and again throughout the book of Acts and the key question the Apostles kept asking was, "Have you received the Spirit?" When we consider the truth that every Christian is a temple of the Spirit, and a priest able to bless others, then having someone lay hands on us and bless us is a powerful experience in which God imparts to us power and the gifts of his Spirit.

Once we are living in the fullness of the Spirit we have to train ourselves to be aware of God's presence with us throughout each day. This is about learning to be in relationship with God in all kinds of different situations. Brother Lawrence wrote about "practising the presence of God". He decided he was going to live as though only he and God were together in the world. He would use the tasks of the day to remind him of God's presence: washing pots represented God cleansing him, polishing silver was God's refining work, gardening linked with the image of God as a gardener. He constantly turned his heart to God throughout his day.

Start to practice this by choosing an hour in your day and try to be aware of God at least once each minute. Or set an alarm for different points in the day and pray. Try living each day with an image of God that will remind you of God's presence or a phrase from his word that you repeat through the day. Or use certain prompts for prayer: each time the phone rings pray for that conversation, when you eat food give thanks, on walks and car journeys turn your thoughts into prayers. Think of how your routines can connect with God's work in you.

Breathe – a rhythm of relationship with God each day
At Holy Trinity we have taught how the image of breathing in and out can give us a picture of a rhythm of relationship with God, allowing his Holy Spirit to fill us as breath fills our lungs. A structure of prayer each day gives deeper points of connection with God, out of which we can live in relationship with him throughout the whole day. Here is the pattern of the Breathe rhythm of daily prayer.

Take a Deep Breath
Having a time devoted to being with God in prayer and reading his word is what Jesus did and it is what all the people who have lived a full and fruitful Christian life have done. There is no other way. So here is a structure for how to spend time with God at the beginning of each day:

IN
How are you?
Is there something you are thankful for?
Take a few minutes to present yourself to God, give thanks for who he is, for all of his blessings and for the day ahead, and be open to his love and presence. Ask for forgiveness for anything that might come between you and him. Worship him and ask for the filling of his Spirit. Breathe in his presence.

UP
Read God's word

Read a passage from the Bible and ask three simple questions:
• What does this teach me about God?
• What does this teach me about people?
• How do I need to respond to this?

OUT

Respond to God's word in prayer: repent, believe, trust. Express thanks, pain or sorrow, questions, hope.

Pray for your personal needs. Pray for the needs of others and those you long to come to faith. Pray for God's help in the day ahead. Ask him what he wants you to do today. Consecrate yourself afresh to him and ask for the Holy Spirit's power to help you represent Jesus today.

Catch your Breath

At different points in the day take time to pray and look for signs of God's kingdom and his presence in the situation you are in. You might like to pray the Lord's Prayer at midday every day, or a time that works for you, as a fixed point of reminder. Questions are a great way to open up relationship with God in the middle of a day such as:
• Lord what does it mean for me to seek your kingdom in this place today?
• Who are you calling me to bless?
• Lord where is your Spirit at work here?

Breathe Out

At the end of each day give time to reflect on the events of the day, to detect God's presence and receive what he wants you to understand from it. As you do this you can entrust all that has happened to God and then rest in God's presence.

Try the structure of prayer below:

1. Become still and aware of God's presence.
2. Review the day with gratitude for his goodness and faithfulness to you throughout this day. Gratitude is the foundation of our relationship with God.
3. As you think about the day, pay attention to your emotions. Reflect on the feelings you experienced during the day. Ask what God is saying through these feelings. Ask forgiveness for your sins. Entrust areas of concern to God.
4. Choose one feature of the day and pray about it. Ask the Holy Spirit to direct you to something during the day that God thinks is particularly important.
5. Look toward tomorrow. Ask God to give you rest and to minister to you as you sleep.

Releasing God's presence:

Praying blessing wherever you go
One of the ways we acknowledge God is with us is to be turning our hearts to him in prayer even when we are with others. I love to *"spread the fragrance of Christ"* (2 Corinthians 2:15) wherever I go, by silently praying blessing over places and people. It is a lovely but simple practice to pray, "Bless them Lord" for each person you meet in a day.

Praying for people when you are with them
The example Jesus gave us and the commission he gave his first disciples was to pray for people and release the healing and freeing presence of God into their lives. There is a great difference between promising to pray for someone at another

time, on your own, and praying *with* them. Both are really helpful and powerful, but praying with them brings them into God's presence in that moment and connects them with him. When you pray with them and they see an answer to that prayer, they connect the answer with the prayer. When we pray separately for someone, God can still answer our prayer but the person often will not see it as God working in their lives. I have done this with people I have visited in their home, workmen who have come to my house, shop workers, people I have been with at weddings or other social occasions.

If you have seen the film *Up* you will remember the scenes where the guard dogs in the film are distracted simply by somebody calling out "Squirrels!" They can't help but respond to this word and search frantically to see if there is a squirrel. This Pavlovian response is automatic because of the connection between the word and their past experience of chasing squirrels.

I want every Christian to have a similarly automatic response whenever someone shares a need with them. As soon as we hear "need" our immediate response should be, 'Can I pray for you?"

We had been doing some training on this with our church leadership team. The next day, David was at the gym when a friend complained about a problem with his shoulder. David immediately thought "need!" and offered to pray. As he prayed for his friend, the pain in his shoulder went.

There is a lot of fear around doing this, most of which comes from our awareness that we are doing something that crosses social boundaries and might seem weird. We worry that we will offend people, or that if nothing happens when we pray we will somehow do more harm than good. Nothing could be further than the truth. Offering to pray with someone is the most loving action we can make in response to hearing of a need. It demonstrates that we care, that we have taken the need seriously. It also shows that we believe what we say.

I was once sharing my faith with a friend called Fiona and she said, "If God is real, then why doesn't he show up and make himself known to me?"

"That's a great question," I said. "Let's pray and see how he wants to show himself to you."

I prayed, asked the Holy Spirit to reveal God's love for her and his presence with us, and then waited. Absolutely nothing happened. I asked if she had felt any sign that God was drawing close to her. Absolutely nothing. I mumbled some explanation about God hearing the prayer and said he would show himself to her in due course, then beat a hasty retreat.

When I got home I ranted at God as I wept in embarrassment and disappointment that I had given God an open goal and he'd missed it. But, within a week Fiona had given her life to Jesus and was wonderfully saved. She later explained that the fact I was willing to pray in such a way was enough evidence that I really believed God was real and this wasn't just an empty religion. God loves to use our failures!

Here is a model to imitate:

Simply ask if you can pray with the person about whatever need they have shared with you. This gives them the opportunity to say no. Even if they do, most people are still really grateful and interested that you wanted to do that. If they say yes, explain that you are going to pray with them now and ask if you can place a hand on their shoulder as a sign of God blessing them. Pray a simple prayer with your eyes open, in such a way that it looks like you're just having a conversation with them. (Don't go all weird and start speaking the language of Zion!)

Here is an example prayer:

Thank you, Lord for, [person's name]
Thank you that you love them
Please (address their need for prayer. If it is physical healing, command healing and speak directly to the condition in Jesus' name. Ask the Holy Spirit to bless them and show them God's love)
Thank you, Lord, for hearing our prayer. I ask all of this for the glory of Jesus and for [name], so that they may know that you love them. Amen.

Then ask them if they felt God doing anything in them while you prayed. They normally do. Even if there is not an immediate answer to the prayer, assure them God has heard them and will bless them. Non-Christians are often much less worried than we are if the prayer isn't answered. They are normally very appreciative of the care you have shown them.

I love Robby Dawkins practice when praying for physical healing, where he asks if the pain or restriction has reduced at all. He asks, "If your pain before I prayed was at level 10, what number would you put it at now?" This is helpful because total healing doesn't always happen immediately and if there is some improvement this raises faith that God is at work and it gives us the opportunity to say, "Can I pray again?"

Elaine is a retired member of Holy Trinity. Her testimony is this:

"As I go about my daily life, I ask the Lord to show me anybody he would like me to talk to or help. On this particular day I was in Asda, doing my weekly shop. I saw an Asian lady, whom I had become friendly with, and she was self-conscious about me seeing her face. I asked if she was alright and she explained that a rash had appeared on her face that was very irritating, red and sore. She had been to the doctors, but they didn't know what it was or what was causing it. I felt the Holy Spirit say, 'Pray for her.' So I explained that I was a Christian, said that Jesus loved her, and that he knew what the problem was, and he could heal it, and would she like me to pray for her. She said yes. As I started to pray, I felt a deep sense of God's presence around us like a bubble. I commanded the rash to go and for healing to come in Jesus' name. After I had prayed, she put her arms around me and thanked me, and said she too felt like we were in a bubble of peace. The next week I met her again in Asda and her face was clear and smooth. She thanked me again and I said it wasn't me, but Jesus, who healed her, and to give him the praise. She also said she knew she was going to be healed after I had prayed. We are now talking about faith and she is open to coming to church."

Sharing Prophetic Words

Paul says *"Eagerly desire spiritual gifts, especially the gift of prophecy."* He explains that the reason gifts of prophecy are so helpful is that they build others up as God gives life-giving words to us to share with them, which comfort, strengthen or encourage them (1 Corinthians 14:1-4). The prophetic word God gives us for non-Christians is often his way of showing that he is real and that he cares for them. It can act like a key to open them to God. When Paul was describing the effect of prophecy on unbelievers who came into a meeting, he explained how it could open them to God's presence, so they saw that, *"God is really among you!"* (1 Corinthians 14:24). All it takes is for us to recognise the voice of God is to consistently ask God to speak to us in the midst of our circumstances and look for patterns of how he begins to speak and guide our thoughts. Asking God to speak creates an expectation that he will, which causes us to "tune in" to what he is saying.

Helen describes her experience of listening to God for one of her colleagues:

"A girl I work with told me that she had a challenging week ahead. In the midst of it she was going to be interviewed at work, along with her colleagues, for a new job they were creating. I told her I would pray for her on the day of the interview. She is a young woman from a strong Christian family, but has gradually drifted away from her own faith. As I began to pray about the demands of the day for her, I had a strong sensation that she was praying for herself. I saw a picture of her praying and golden glitter was falling on her face and covering her skin. I changed my prayers to worship and asked God for her to feel his love and bless her with an experience of his Holy Spirit, just as I was having then. I was able to talk to her about this and we continued to talk about this and faith."

So while at work, with friends, in a meeting, or praying for someone, you can quietly pray something like,

"Is there anything you want to say to me about this Lord?"

"Father, what do you love about this person?"

"Lord, I seek your wisdom about this..."

"Lord, please give me a word to share with this person."

Then we listen, looking for a thought that comes into our mind, an image in our imagination, or an intuitive sense of what God is saying to us. Check to see if it is from God (does it glorify him? Does it agree with Scripture? Do you have an inner conviction or peace about it? What will be the fruit of sharing it with the person?) Talk to God about whatever you think he is saying. Ask questions about it. Ask for greater clarity. Ask him to help you know what he is wanting you to do with it.

Now share it with the person, gently suggesting God is speaking to you about their situation. Do this with love and humility, and if it is from God it will bring great blessing to them. If it's not from God it will easily be forgotten.

Simon tells the story of when he was doing some shopping in Leicester city centre:

"I was walking through our city centre when my heart was drawn to a man leaning against a monument in the city centre. He had a shaved head and was covered in tattoos and had several piercings on his face. I confess that I didn't like the look of him. I felt the Lord say, 'Go over to that man and tell him I will never beat him like his Father did.' To be honest I wasn't keen to obey, but I chose to trust that this was what God wanted me to do. I walked over to him and said,

'Hi, my name's Simon and I'm a minister in this city and God talks to me about people. He told me to come to you and tell that you he will never beat you like your father did.' The guy got very angry clenched his fists and swore at me a few times, but then suddenly his eyes filled with tears and he said, 'How did you know my dad did that?' I told him, 'I didn't know that, but God does and he loves you so much that he told a stranger to come and tell you he loves you and won't beat you, and that you will be safe with him because he knows you and cares about you.' The man sobbed on my shoulder and a member of a local church team who happened to be in the city centre ministered to him."

My best experience of this was when I was walking my dog. As I walked past a young woman I prayed God's blessing over her and I felt God say to me, "Speak to her about her destiny." I immediately thought, "What on earth does that mean?" As I was thinking this, she had walked off and I definitely didn't want to stalk her round the park. So I said to God, "If I see her again, I'll stop and talk to her and trust that you will help me know what I'm meant to say."

I almost completed my circuit of the park and was feeling a little glad that I hadn't seen her again. But then my dog stopped to relieve himself and after I'd cleared it up I saw her. Imagine the scene: me with a bag of dog's mess in my hand going up to her and saying, "Hi, sorry to disturb you, but while I walk around here with my dog I pray, and when I saw you earlier I felt God speak to me about you. He says he has really good plans for you in the future and it is going to be okay." She immediately started to cry and explained that she had come to this country from South Africa to be with her boyfriend, but he had just ended the relationship and she was walking around the park feeling that she had ruined her life and what on earth was she going to do. I prayed for her for God's help and blessing.

PRESS PLAY

In the Christian community you are part of, you will need to find opportunities to pray for others and to listen to God for each other. If you don't do this with Christian friends you will never do it with people you meet outside of church. As you do this together, ask others to pray for the Holy Spirit to fill you and empower you.

Each day begin to practice being aware of God's presence with you. Start to ask God questions during the day about what he is doing and what he wants to say to you. Ask God to give you an opportunity to pray with someone and keep praying for that until you do.

Individual / Group Study
IN

How are you?

Is there something you are thankful for?

When have you experienced God speaking to you outside of a church meeting?

UP

Read Mark 6:30-44

What does this teach us about God?

(Think about his compassion, willingness to bless, the abundance of the food etc.)

What does this teach us about people?

(Take Jesus' example of a human being in relationship with his Father. What does he give us as an example to follow in the way he responds to the lack of food? What do the disciples teach us?)

How do you need to respond?

OUT

Prayerfully think about what you will be doing in the coming week. Ask God to meet you in these places and to give you courage to join in with what he is doing there.

Commit to start each day in the coming week with a prayer for opportunities to bless and pray for people.

3
Asking Questions / Telling Stories: the art of loving conversation

Introduction

"And pray for us, too, that God may open a door for our message, so that we may proclaim the mystery of Christ, for which I am in chains. Pray that I may proclaim it clearly, as I should. Be wise in the way you act toward outsiders; make the most of every opportunity. Let your conversation be always full of grace, seasoned with salt, so that you may know how to answer everyone." (Colossians 4:2-6)

Many social commentators lament how the art of conversation is being lost as people prefer to use email, texts and tweets to communicate. "Can we talk?" has become one of the most pressing social, cultural, even philosophical issues of our day. It's not that social media can't be a tool for good and a great way of staying in touch. But the Gospel needs to be spoken about and the Christians I know seem to feel that "breaking the sound barrier" really is as hard as it sounds.

Have you ever been asked a question that changed your perspective or opened up your heart to something you hadn't been aware of before? I know I have. The art of conversation requires two primary skills: asking questions and listening.

These are both expressions of love. Most people love to talk about themselves and so the gift of someone who is interested in us and willing to listen is a gift of love. The connection that takes place between two people in conversation can be profound and conversation is how relationships are built. This is *Mission-Shaped Grace*.

When we reframe evangelism so that we understand it as *asking questions* and *telling stories* we step away from formulaic and programmatic approaches and place the proclamation of the Gospel back in the context of loving relationship. We ask questions because we love and care for that person and we want to know them better. Asking a question is like building a bridge into somebody's heart and soul – it opens them up for you to build a deeper friendship and to show them that you care for them as you know more about them. It also opens them up to God as they share more of who they are and what they think.

As people answer questions we discover how the Good News is relevant to them. We can then tell the story of the Gospel, or our testimony, in ways that connect with them. We love stories in our culture. Rather than making blunt statements of doctrinal truth that shut down conversations, stories invite people to explore them.

Last year I visited Holy Island, Lindisfarne. This was the centre of the monastic community which St Aidan founded in AD635 and which St Cuthbert then led. The story goes that Aidan brought twelve monks from the Island of Iona at the request of King Oswald, and chose the island of Lindisfarne as the centre for his mission. Historians describe how Aidan would then leave the island and walk from one village to another, having conversations with the people he saw and slowly interesting them in Christianity. He deliberately didn't travel on horseback because he wanted the chance to meet people and talk with them about faith. By patiently talking to people on their level, and by taking an active interest in their lives and communities, Aidan and his monks slowly restored Christianity to the Northumbrian countryside. In his years of evangelism, Aidan was responsible for the construction of churches, monasteries and schools throughout Northumbria and had a reputation for generously caring for the poor.

The pattern of mission from this period of history, before we created parishes and thousands of church buildings, have much to teach us about our missionary context today. The pattern Aidan established was a church centre as a place of sending out and returning from mission. That is what our churches have to become: we gather to be renewed through God's word, his Spirit and Christian community. But as we part, we go with a sense of being commissioned to proclaim the Gospel.

On Sundays we sometimes use this blessing to send people out and commission God's people on mission:

All: I have been crucified with Christ and I no longer live, but Christ lives in me. The life I now live in the body, I live by faith in the Son of God, who loved me and gave himself for me.

Leader: You are an ambassador of Jesus Christ. Wherever you go, God is sending you; wherever you are, God has a purpose in your being there. Christ, who indwells you, has something he wants to do through you. Believe this and receive the blessing of his empowering presence. Go in peace to love and serve the Lord.

All: In the name of Christ. Amen!

Principle

This is what Jesus did. He asked questions and told stories. There are over 100 questions that Jesus asked recorded in the gospels. He would even answer questions with a question. We need to pay attention to this because he is the truth of God. If anyone could have confidence to simply to declare the truth, it was Jesus. He clearly taught about the kingdom, but much of this was done in parables. We need to learn how to have faith-filled conversations with questions and stories that open people up to God.

In John 4 Jesus meets a Samaritan woman and starts a conversation with her by asking a question: *"Will you give me a drink?"* This was a risky question because Jesus was crossing social and racial boundaries. But the question led to Jesus telling a story about the type of water that, after drinking it, you are never thirsty again. He invited the woman to explore this idea with him. And we know the story about how this led to her and her village coming to faith in him. All from a question and a story.

The questions we need to ask are ones that open people up, not close things down. They need to come out of love for the person and a genuine interest in them. If we love someone, the greatest gift we can give them is to accompany them along their journey of coming to faith in Jesus. This leads us to the stories we need to tell: our story and God's story. Our story is our story of faith – how we came to faith, but also current stories that show the difference God makes to our life. God's story is the Gospel story of a God of love wanting relationship with the whole world that had rejected him and all he did to make this possible.

Presence

The really interesting part of the story of Jesus and the Samaritan woman is how the Holy Spirit prompts Jesus to ask a challenging question: "Why don't you go and get your husband?" "I have no husband," she replies and Jesus is able to reveal the prophetic knowledge he has about her life. We are invited to live the life Jesus lived. He showed us that questions and stories create space in relationships for God to come into. This again requires us to do the job of double-listening: listening to the person and listening to God, and asking him to show us anything he wants about that person.

Practice

Recently, we had a team lead a united churches mission on the streets of Leicester. It involved them teaching us a very tight evangelistic script which we could use to lead people through a conversation to come to a point where they could receive prayer and respond to God themselves in prayer. Almost 600 people prayed with us and again we discovered that the fields are ripe for harvest. I confess that I didn't like the script, but one of the big lessons God was teaching us was that having a form of words that people could learn gave them the confidence to go out onto the streets and talk to complete strangers. Over 150 people did this, many of whom were people I would never have imagined being able to do this.

The aim of *Mission-Shaped Grace* is to give you practices that will give you confidence to share Jesus with your friends, colleagues and family, and although we are looking for long term and natural friendships and conversations, this section will give you some words to use which I hope will give you confidence to share the Gospel with others.

Asking Questions

Asking Questions of God
Here are some great questions to use as you do that "double-listening" and engage with God as you meet with someone:
• What do you love about this person?
• What are you wanting to do in this person's life?
• What do you want to show me about this person, Lord?
• How can I serve them Lord?

Asking Questions of Others
The questions we may ask another person depend on the context and relationship we have with them. But the key to asking the right question that will build our relationship with that person is to listen to them. Listen to what they say and remember it! Show your interest by your body language and verbal affirmation of what they have said. Don't interrupt in order to say what you want to tell them – wait and genuinely respond to what you have heard.

Often the questions that build a relationship and open someone to God are the courageous questions. People talk about having the last 10% of the conversation – asking the question you know you should ask, that needs to be asked, but that you also know will touch some pain, or will uncover something, or might challenge and produce a strong reaction.

There is a time for questions. There is a time for giving answers and the reason for the hope within us. But there is a time for questions. When questions are raised at the right time, the search for answers can move a person forward in their journey to faith in giant leaps. Questions are also a much softer way of engaging people in talking about Jesus than simply telling them about our faith. Questions such as:

- Would you like to come to ... with me?
- Do you feel near or far from God?
- I wasn't always a Christian. Would you like to hear how I came to follow Jesus? (then tell your story)
- I sometimes meet up with people to talk about life and faith and look at a story from Jesus' life together. Would you like to do that with me?
- Where are you in your spiritual journey? ... What do you know about Jesus? ... Could I show you something that really helps me to understand what is so important about Jesus? (share the Gospel with them using something like the 3 Circles presentation explained later in this chapter)
- What do you think the biggest barrier is to you believing in God?

These questions are just examples of how to ask questions that get people talking about God and faith, and which then give you the opportunity to share something with them. And you will be able to come up with your own version of these questions that are much better suited to your "voice" and your friends. Asking the right next question is the key to linking a conversation you have about God, or a moment when you prayed with a friend, or a generous act which has touched them, to God himself. Thinking strategically is important. Actually, the most important question is one that you ask yourself: "What would the best next step be for this person on their journey to faith?" Then plan to help them have that opportunity.

Telling Stories:

Sharing your story
"'Return home and tell how much God has done for you.' So
the man went away and told all over town how much Jesus
had done for him." (Luke 8:39)

Sharing your story can help family, friends, and people you meet understand how they too can follow Jesus. They are interested in you, and what matters to you matters to them. Your story is also helpful because they need examples of how people go on a journey to faith in Christ. i.e. people aren't born as Christians, but over the course of our lives our faith and relationship with God develops. And because it has happened for you, it can happen for them. Don't forget the principle of vulnerability: share some stuff that isn't perfect about you, so they don't think you have to be perfect in order to be a Christian. In a moment we'll look at how to share the "big" story of you coming to faith. But a testimony can also include something like an answer to prayer, a great experience at church, or the difference God made to a difficult situation. These "small" stories can often be easier to drop naturally into conversation or to relate to something one of your friends is going through. Here are some tips on how to do it:

- Don't use religious language
- Don't go into too much of the detail of the story
- Don't focus exclusively on *you*. Ultimately you are seeking to point to Jesus
- Keep it short – 2-3 minutes

Write down a few points under each heading.

1. *Your life before you met Jesus.* "There was a time in my life when..." (Describe the main factors you were dealing with that led to you opening your life to Jesus).

2. *How you met Jesus.* "Then I decided to..." (Describe how you came to ask God to forgive you, decided to follow Jesus and the difference it made immediately).

3. *How your life has changed.* "And now the difference Jesus has made to my life is..." (Say how God has changed your life, but be authentic in sharing the struggles as well as the joys).

At the end of sharing this, ask a question. "Where are you in your spiritual journey?" or "Thanks for listening. What does that make you think about?" or "Would you like me to explain how you can come close to God?"

I remember when I was having a coffee with my friend Chris. We were sitting next to the shop door and people were going in and out of the door to have a smoke. I grumbled about it, but then admitted that I had smoked when I was eleven. He was surprised and asked me what was going on in my life at that time. This gave me the chance to share how I was rebelling against my Christian upbringing and then I told him my story of coming to faith and the difference Jesus had made to my life. When I had finished he was visibly moved by what I'd shared and said, "That is what I want to happen for me." Chris has since come to faith and the transformation in his life has been wonderful to see.

PRESS PLAY

Practising telling your story may seem a really simple thing to do, but you will be surprised how easy it is to get sidetracked or use religious language, or not be very clear about what Jesus has done for you. Practising it also releases faith that you are going to share it with someone. So write out the basics of your story. Practice telling your story in three minutes with a Christian friend. Then think about who will you share your story with this week. Commit to doing it and tell someone who will help you to be accountable. Now pray for an opportunity and plan the best way to lead into a conversation in which you share your story.

Sharing God's story

Together with your own story, you need to be able to share the gospel story with your friends, family and the people you meet. After you have asked one of the above questions and are having a conversation with someone, or you have prayed with someone, you need to create a "bridge" from that into a conversation about God's story, the Gospel. Here are a few examples of bridge questions:

- Family and friends of a new disciple: "I have made a decision to become a follower of Jesus. Can I tell you about it?"
- Someone you meet: "If you could know God personally, would you be interested in me telling you how?"
- Anyone: "Do you feel near or far from God? Could I share with you how you could come close to him?"

Once someone has said "yes" to any of those questions, you

then have to know what to do! So first of all, here is a great way to share the message of the Gospel that Jimmy Scroggins, a pastor at First Baptist Church, West Palm Beach, Florida, has developed called *The Three Circles*.

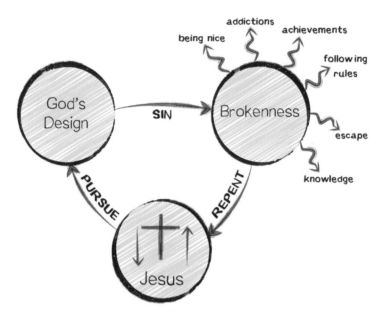

While drawing it, you could say something like this (but again, find the words and way to use this tool that fit you):

"So, we live in a broken world. When we look around, or watch the news, we see messed up stuff everywhere. Awful things happen to people: murder, theft, depression. I'm the same. There have been loads of things that I've done that are just plain bad (you can share something of your story here if you think it will help). I'm sure you can think of some for yourself, too.

But, if we see brokenness in this world, we also see goodness and beauty. It might be the laughter of a child or

153

the beauty of a sunrise, but there are definitely some amazing things in this world. That's because we can still see the evidence of God's design for this world. When he made it, it was good, and the plan was that we would live with him in this world forever, and he has a design for the best way to live in every area of our lives: family life, work, relationships, how we handle money, sex, power.

But we thought we knew a better way than his design and turned our backs on him. We rejected God's plan for how it would all work. The Bible uses the word 'sin' to describe this rebellion. So we find ourselves knee deep in our sin and brokenness, and we want to get out of it, but we can't. People try all sorts of things to deal with that sense of brokenness. They try to numb the pain with alcohol or buying things to make them feel better. They try to earn loads of money or do good deeds in the hope it will make the feeling of brokenness go away. They even try attending church or following a religion. Well, each of these things is like a bungee cord and, though we get a little further away from our sin and brokenness, it doesn't deal with the problem and we soon get pulled back into it again.

God knew we were in this mess, and didn't want to leave us like that, because if we stay separated from God then it lasts for eternity. So, He came in the person of his Son, Jesus. He lived a perfect life, but then he died on a cross to pay for all our sin and brokenness, and then he rose from the grave in order to make a new kind of life possible for all of us. He said that if we turn and believe in him, putting our trust in him and following him with our lives, then we could begin to recover and to pursue God's good plan for our lives."

At the end of sharing this presentation of the Gospel the

key is to ask three great questions: 1) *So, where do you think you are in this picture?* Over here, just enjoying God's design, or are you over here, feeling a bit stuck in brokenness? Or have you accepted God's offer of forgiveness and freedom and are pursuing life with Jesus? 2) *Where would you like to be?* And 3) *Is there anything stopping you accepting Jesus' gift of forgiveness and new life now?*

At that point you can pray with the person and ask them to pray with you.

Here's a great story of how learning the Three Circles tool equipped a person to lead someone to faith in Jesus:

Sarah came to faith on an Alpha course and was being mentored by Pep in how to follow Jesus and make other disciples. Sarah had been praying for her neighbour, Steph, and helping her with her disabled daughter, and she got to know Steph's brother, Gary. One day, when Gary was waiting for Steph outside the flat, Sarah invited him in to wait inside. She had been doing a Bible study and invited Gary to join her. That began a journey for Gary and he subsequently gave his life to Jesus. Steph had been quite antagonistic towards Sarah (because she knew Sarah was a Christian and Steph was a Wiccan witch). However, after Gary became a Christian, Steph noticed the change in him and started to talk to Sarah more about spiritual things.

When Pep was visiting Sarah for a mentoring session, she suggested they invite Steph up for a coffee. She was free and came straight up. They were chatting about the difficulties Steph was facing and life in general when Pep felt a prompt from the Holy Spirit to explain the Gospel and what Steph needed to do to be saved. This is how Pep described it:

"I wasn't very keen, as I thought it was a bit of a gear change, and I didn't want to spoil Sarah's good work with Steph by being too pushy. But the feeling I ought to do it remained, so I asked Steph if I could explain to her why Jesus had come into the world. I grabbed a bit a paper and a pen and talked her through the Three Circles diagram we'd all been taught how to do in church. I hadn't done it for a while, so I forgot bits of it, but it seemed to make sense to Steph because when I got to the end and asked her where she felt she was, she answered without hesitation that she was still in the brokenness part, but that she wanted to move back towards God's plan for her life and for healing and restoration. I told her that she could do that very easily, simply by thanking God for all he'd done for her, asking forgiveness for the way she had led her life, and surrendering her life to him and asking him to come and live in her by the Holy Spirit to help her to be his disciple. Because she'd been a witch, she understood a lot about spiritual realities, but I wasn't sure she'd completely understood what being a disciple of Jesus might mean for her. I asked her if she needed time to think about it, but she was certain she wanted to pray right then, so I led her in a simple prayer. When we got to the bit asking for God's forgiveness, I asked her if there was anything particular she wanted forgiveness for and asked God to speak to her. The answer she gave left me in no doubt that God was revealing his heart to her and that she was absolutely right about the timing!"

After Sarah and Pep had both prayed for her to receive the Holy Spirit (which happened really gently and beautifully), Steph asked if they would go and pray in her flat. She'd had a number of unwelcome spiritual disturbances, probably due to her past interest in the occult, and she wanted it to stop. They grabbed some oil from the kitchen and blessed it in Jesus' name, then went down to her flat, where they prayed over the whole flat and told the unwanted spirits to leave in Jesus' name, then anointed both Steph and the room with the oil. The atmosphere in the flat completely changed and Steph said that she saw the spirit leave. She confirmed later that it had never returned (although Steph needed further prayer sessions to help her to overcome some of the issues of her past). Steph then got rid of all the things she had that were related to occult spiritual practices.

This is a great example of how a couple of simple questions, an invite for coffee, and a question about whether she would like to know more about Jesus, opened up the fact that Steph was hungry to know God and ready to believe in Jesus. But it was only because Pep had practised using the Three Circles tool that she was ready when the opportunity came.

PRESS PLAY

Yes it's practice time again! Grab a piece of paper and practise drawing the three circles from memory. See what you can remember and what you have forgotten. Then draw it again and try to describe what it means, explaining the Gospel as you do it. Over the next week, practice doing it once every day – while you're having lunch, on the train to work, or whenever you have five minutes spare. Keep on practising until you become confident with it. Now pray for an opportunity to use it.

Sharing God's stories

Think about the great stories Jesus told. A great way to connect people with God is to use his word and allow it to speak to them. Read the following Bible passages listed in the next section and learn the stories. They will probably be familiar to you, but you'll be surprised at how poorly you can recall them unless you choose to learn them. When you're in a conversation with someone, think about which story would help them to engage with God and ask them if you can share it with them. Or when you ask someone to meet up with you to look at stories from Jesus' life, use them in what people have termed "Discovery Bible Study".

Meeting to read Gospel stories with someone is the best way to lead them to put their faith in Jesus, because God's word is powerful. Look for an appropriate time to ask the key question, "Would you like to meet up to talk about faith and look at what the Bible tells us about Jesus?" I know you think that everyone you know will say "no" to such a cringey question! But actually they won't, because I thought the same until I persuaded myself to make the invitation to a friend. I even practiced it in front of a mirror and told myself I was not allowed to go home until I had asked him. He said "yes".

So if one of your friends says "yes", will you know what to do? Discovery Bible Study follows the pattern that we have been using for our individual or group studies at the end of each section. Wherever you are and whatever passage of Scripture or story from Jesus' life you are looking at, you can now share one-to-one with someone or lead a small discussion group using the same simple pattern. So learn the pattern and read the passages.

IN

How are you doing?
Is there something you are thankful for?
What did you learn last time?
What did you do about what you learned?
Did you talk about it with anyone else?

UP

Read the story
Retell the passage in your own words to check that they have understood it.
What does the passage teach us about God or Jesus?
What does it teach us about people?
How do you need to respond to it?

OUT

What will you do this week to respond to what you have learned?
Who could you tell the story to this week?
How can we pray for each other?

Seven stories of hope:
1. The woman who wept at Jesus' feet (Luke 7:36-50)
2. Accepted by God (Luke 18:9-17)
3. A hole in the roof (Luke 5:17-26)
4. Two lost sons (Luke 15:11-32)
5. Death and forgiveness (Mark 15-16-39)
6. New life, new purpose (Matthew 28:1–20)
7. Which soil are you? (Mark 4:1-20)

If you are sharing these stories with someone who doesn't

know Jesus, at some point you can ask them where they are with God, and use the three circles to check if they are ready to put their faith in Jesus.

PRESS PLAY:

Take some time to review your progress:
How are you getting on praying for your non-Christian friends every day?
Are you feeding on God's word and praying to be filled with the Holy Spirit every day?
Have you taken an opportunity to pray or share with someone?
Have you learned your story and the Three Circles Gospel presentation? How confident do you feel if you had the chance to use them?
Now learn one of the Gospel stories listed and pray for an opportunity to share it with a Christian friend this week. Share how your progress is going and ask them to pray for you and hold you accountable in your next step in mission and using the *Grace Notes* tools.

Individual / Group Study
IN

How are you?
Is there something you are thankful for?
When did you last have a significant conversation with a friend about God or faith?

UP

Read John 4:1-26
What does this teach us about God?
(Look at Jesus' example of reaching out to this woman)

What does this teach us about people?
(Look at how this woman responded to Jesus)
How do you need to respond?

OUT

Look at the action points and think about who you can tell
your story or God's story to this week.

4
Calling:
finding your unique "shape" and contribution to God's mission

Introduction

When Jesus called Peter, James and John to follow him he said, *"Come follow me and I will teach you to fish for people"* (Matthew 4:19). He did that because they were fishermen. I don't think he was saying that fishing is the perfect metaphor for mission. I think he was saying something like, "You know how to fish for fish. Well, you're just the kind of person I need in my mission team because we're going to be fishing for people." In his parables, Jesus used farming analogies to describe the kingdom, so my guess is that if Peter, James and John had been farmers, he would have said, "Come and follow me and I will teach you how to grow disciples." He was using their language and affirming their abilities and he wants to do that with us. Today, to the salesperson, he would say, "Come follow me and I will teach you how to 'sell' the Gospel message" or to the computer programmer "Come and follow me and I will teach you how to solve the problems that stop people coming to me" or to a baker, "Come and follow me and I will teach you the recipe for making disciples."

Each of us is unique. Our uniqueness will affect how we most naturally engage with God's call to make disciples, and it will also affect how we connect with different people who are not yet Christians. But what people often do is to use their uniqueness to excuse them from being involved in making disciples. They say, "It's not my gift to share the Gospel with others" or "I'm an introvert. I can't be an extrovert evangelist like you" or "I don't feel called to evangelism." Such statements show a misunderstanding of calling. We have to hold together two opposing truths:

(i) **Diversity:** the truth that each of us is unique and given unique gifts by the Holy Spirit and a different calling within the mission of God

(ii) **Unity:** the truth that the same Holy Spirit fills each one of us and calls every one of us to be a witness and represent Jesus Christ and his kingdom in this world

Each Christian has been given a *general* and a *specific* calling. Our general calling includes everything that every baptised Christian is instructed to do in the New Testament. This is the general grace of God. But each of us is a different "shape" with a specific grace that will affect our natural missional approach. Our specific calling connects with the unique personality, gifting and abilities God has put within us.

I heard of one older woman who had been encouraged to take part in some evangelism on the streets, but she really didn't like the training she received. When the teams went onto the streets she said to God that she wasn't going to take part and she hoped he was OK with this. But because she didn't want to discourage the others, she went out and sat on a bench and prayed for the team. While she did this, a young woman next to her on the bench. They started a conversation which gave the woman an opportunity to pray with this girl. So, in fact, she discovered that she *could* do evangelism, but that God would use her in the way he knew worked for her.

I think that one of the reasons why many of us feel inadequate in evangelism is because the models that have been held up as good examples are so different from us – the evangelist who leads thousands to Christ from a stage, the gifted healer who demonstrates the kingdom so powerfully, or those who seem able to walk up to anyone and start a conversation about faith immediately.

We are definitely not all like that, but we are all called and commissioned to make disciples. We never win in the game of comparison – we are either left feeling inadequate and discouraged, unable to match up to the model presented, or we end up trying harder and harder to be someone we were never meant to be, and so miss the gifts God has given us, and the way in which he wants to use us.

It reminds me of the moment when David's life was in the greatest danger. It was when he offered to fight Goliath and was presented to King Saul. Saul imposed on him his "missional shape". In other words, he insisted that David must be dressed in the best armour and given the biggest, best sword. But when David put on Saul's armour he was almost immobilised by its weight. In that moment his life hangs in the balance. Is he going to obediently wear armour that doesn't fit and make himself a sitting duck? Fortunately he says, "I can't go out in these," takes the armour off and picks up five stones and his sling-shot. He knows how he can fulfil the mission he senses God's call to. He knows how his past experience has shaped and prepared him.

As we learn the other missional tools, this section gives us the opportunity to think about different approaches and how our uniqueness might affect how we will use them to share our faith.

Principle

Listen to how Paul explains this in his letter to the Ephesians:

"There is one body and one Spirit, just as you were called to one hope when you were called; one Lord, one faith, one baptism; one God and Father of all, who is over all and through all and in all. But to each one of us grace has been given as Christ apportioned it ... Christ himself gave some to be apostles, some to be prophets, some to be evangelists, and some to be pastors and teachers, to equip his people for works of service, so that the body of Christ may be built up until we all reach unity in the faith and in the knowledge of the Son of God and become mature, attaining to the whole measure of the fullness of Christ." (Ephesians 4:4-13)

Before we go on to talk about unique gifting, let us first acknowledge our common calling.

"...there is one..." We are united in our calling in the Holy Spirit under God's authority. Contained within our baptism is our commissioning and authorisation as Christ's ambassadors and witnesses. I want to make sure that regardless of our personality type or spiritual gifts we accept we are all called to be disciples who make disciples. This is discipleship 101. The mission God has called us all on is one of personal obedience to the same God and Father of all, wherever we are. But Paul is clear that, *"...to each one of us grace has been given as Christ apportioned it."* There are several other passages in the New Testament that teach about the grace God gives to individuals in order to serve him.

These specific "graces" are called spiritual gifts and vary from gifts of healing to gifts of helping and administration. These are like the tools a workman has in his toolbox to help him get the job done. My understanding is that these tools are available to all of us, according to what we need to serve God. We can all prophecy at times, we can all heal the sick, we can all share the Bible with someone, and we can all experience the compassion God gives us for someone.

But as well as having the toolkit the Holy Spirit provides for all of us, God also gives a specific anointing, an intensified gifting, in a certain area of ministry that helps us understand what he is calling us to do in his service. In effect, this is our main "job" in the kingdom – our base camp. It doesn't restrict us from involvement in other areas, but our base camp is where we fit and are most fruitful. We can all heal the sick, but some have been given the gift of healings in greater intensity and permanency, to strengthen the church's ministry in this area. Because of this, God uses them consistently in healing others. We can all prophecy, but prophets will have an intensified version of this gift that will strengthen this ministry in the whole church. We can all love and care for people, but pastors have grace to gather and call others to care and guide and support God's people.

"To each one of us..." Everyone has been given one or more of these ministry gifts, not just a select few, and not just the public leaders or the church staff. Everyone! Including you! This passage teaches us that every one of us has a role. Paul then describes five leadership roles that Jesus has given to the Church: apostle, prophet, evangelist, pastor, teacher. These five roles enable the whole Church to be strengthened and everyone to be equipped to be involved in God's mission.

Together they describe the full ministry of Jesus: he was apostolic because he had been sent from heaven and lived constantly on mission in the power of the Spirit. One of his titles is "prophet" and he clearly heard his Father speak to him and was led by the Spirit. He was an amazing teacher, teaching unlike anyone people had ever heard, as he taught with authority. Jesus demonstrated his pastoral care and compassion and declared that he is the Good Shepherd. And wherever he went, he proclaimed the good news of the kingdom – he was an evangelist. Therefore the Church that is his body on earth today must reflect these different graces and ministries.

This doesn't mean that all of us will become church leaders in these roles. But it is logical to conclude that if these five roles can equip the whole Church, each of us has been gifted and called to serve God within one of these five general areas. And from this it can be helpful to reflect on which one you fit best within. Paul says that the ministry area has been determined by the *"grace that has been given as Christ apportioned it."* So the type and measure of your gift has been determined by Jesus. Your responsibility is to understand what he has given you and be faithful with it. Two things follow from understanding this:

1. It will help you to understand how you will naturally do mission – what your missional shape is.
2. It will guide you in what your contribution to the church's general life and ministry should be. As Paul explains, *"to equip his people for works of service, so that the body of Christ may be built up until we all reach unity in the faith and in the knowledge of the Son of God and become mature, attaining to the whole measure of the fullness of*

Christ." It's all for others and for God's glory and so we need to avoid being precious and self-promoting as we discern these things.

This book is about missional practices, so it is beyond its scope to give much time to thinking about our place of service within the church. But it is a useful point to note that mission is never an individualistic activity. When Jesus talked about fishing for people, he had a net with a boat of fishermen in mind, not a solitary figure with a rod on a riverbank. Not everyone on a lifeboat has the same job, but everyone has the same goal which, in the words of the RNLI mission statement, is to *"save lives at sea"*.

In church, no one person has got it altogether, but altogether every person has got it! Jesus has shaped us to fit best in a particular place and role within his Church, where his grace can flow in us and through us as we serve him. This is good news because it means that God does not expect you to be someone you are not. He does, however, want you to be all that he made you to be. So within the Christian community that you are part of, you will contribute differently, and together you will disciple people and see more disciples made.

God has made each one of us uniquely, with a different combination of natural abilities, spiritual gifts and our personalities. There is real grace in discovering that we don't have to be someone we're not, because it saves us from comparing ourselves with others, and experiencing disappointment, failure or frustration as we try harder and harder to do something we will never succeed in doing.

It also means we don't have be multi-talented and do

everything. We simply have to find a place where we fit.

Presence

As we have just said, it is the Holy Spirit who works these gifts and graces in our lives. They don't arrive as fully developed tools to simply slot into our lives. They require us to cooperate with God, to begin to serve, and to see what we find the flow of the Spirit in. Pray for the Holy Spirit's filling and for him to show you what ministry gift he has given you. As you focus on areas in which he has gifted you, you will find it easier to flow with the Spirit because you aren't going against the grain. Instead you are flowing in the direction of how he has made you and what he has called you to do.

Practice

Finding your calling or your "missional shape" is not an academic exercise, but one of trying different things and reflecting. As someone has said, it is much easier to steer a moving car than a stationary one. Likewise, it is much easier to discover God's calling when we are already on the move and actively involved in some way, as opposed to sitting and waiting for God to show us before we start to serve.

How you will be most fruitful in mission will be affected by your personality type, spiritual gifts, abilities and experience. All these factors affect your "shape". In order to give you a framework which is simple enough for you to work with, we will focus on the five-fold ministry gifts. On the following pages are descriptions of each gift. They contain a general description that will help you consider where you might be called to serve within the church. But the main aim is to help you find out how the way in which God has gifted you will shape your approach to mission. You may find that you fit with more than one area and most people find this. But it is helpful to try and find one or two areas that you think best describe you.

Ministry Areas

Apostle

The word apostle literally means one who is "sent out". Pioneering new mission and strategically directing the life of the church, or a part of the church, apostles are people who like to start new things. They see change as a good thing and they are often people who are always on the move and can't sit still. In business, they are entrepreneurs, coming up with new opportunities and products. They love dreaming dreams. In the Bible, Jesus' disciples were the first apostles. Jesus "sent them out" and they didn't sit around in Jerusalem for very long – they went out into the known world planting churches. Paul was also one of the first apostles and he was the most effective church planter and missionary the early Church had. These first apostles were unique in that they had seen Jesus and were given authority to write God's word as they recalled Jesus' life, so that the Gospels were written and the Church was strengthened by their writings.

But the role of apostle is still one that God needs within his Church. In the church in Rome that Paul started we find reference to Priscilla and Aquilla, who helped Paul plant new churches. In Romans Paul also says, *"Andronicus and Junia, my fellow Jews who have been in prison with me. They are outstanding among the apostles"* (Romans 16:7).

In church, this gift of pioneering, pushing forward, stepping out beyond the current patterns of doing things, can be seen in any ministry. E.g. starting a missional community, developing a new way of reaching out to friends, creating a new pattern of youth ministry, etc. If this is your calling then you will notice this through your personality traits, or in the way that God has put dreams or desires to change things, or to do something new for him, in your heart.

When it comes to sharing faith with others, you will enjoy innovating and trying new things. You will probably be up for going out on the streets, as well as sharing with friends. You will often be able to identify the next step that will help your friend come closer to faith and strategically create opportunities to talk about faith with them.

Your problem will be having enough patience to walk with your friend as they move towards faith in Christ. You can see the way the missional tools will help you to lead people to faith, but you will want to develop your own formats. You will identify most with Jesus on mission when he breaks new ground, such as when he sends the 72 out into new territory (Luke 10).

My experience of being apostolic on mission has been that my strategic gift helps me to understand where my friends are in their spiritual journey, and to choose the right moment to bring the challenge or suggestion of what their next step might be.

Prophet

Prophetic ministry involves listening to God. Prophets enjoy spending time with God in prayer and have an ability to discern what the Spirit is saying to them. They will often have an inner understanding given to them by the Holy Spirit of what God is doing now and what he is wanting to do in the future.

This is a gift to the church, as it allows leaders to step back and consider the broader perspective of what God is doing. Prophets listen to God on behalf of others and communicate what God is saying to them. In this way prophets strengthen and encourage others, giving them confidence to step into the future God is calling them to. The prophetic personality is often intuitive and creative, and comonly produces artists, musicians and poets.

In the Old Testament there were a few very significant people who were recognised in the role of prophet. In the New Testament this role opens up to many different people and there are numerous examples: Anna and Simeon prophesy over Jesus as a newborn baby. In Acts 11:28 Agabus predicts a severe famine and later, in Acts 21:11, he takes hold of Paul's belt and prophesies his future imprisonment. Philip's daughters are known as prophetesses (Acts 21:9). As a prophetic person you will be able to relate to Jesus' mission when he is releasing the Spirit's power in healing or prophecy, such as when he speaks prophetically to Nathanael and turns him from a sceptic into a believer (John 1).

On mission you can ask God to give you revelation about the person you are sharing with. Or, as you pray for your five friends, God will give you understanding of what to pray and what might be holding them back from seeking him.

There is, however, the temptation for you to avoid using practical tools, such as those contained in this book, as you naturally rely on responding to the leading of the Spirit. Some advice from the life of the great revivalist, John Wesley: he was once told to stop proclaiming the Gospel wherever he went, and encouraged to only speak to those people the Holy Spirit told him to. He recorded in his journal the next day after trying this approach, "Spoke to no one. Going back to old methods."

You can use the tools to create a structure for you to build disciple-making relationships with people, and then use your prophetic gift to open up those people to God. You might do this through sharing a word directly with someone, or using the revelation the Holy Spirit gives to guide your conversation with, or prayers for, them. Maybe you are not at the place where you can confidently call yourself a prophet, but prayer and seeking God are what causes your soul to sing, and you naturally find the Receiving and Releasing God's Presence tool a good fit for you – so go for it.

My friend Simon, who I mentioned earlier, is a gifted prophet and he does evangelism using prophetic revelation. An example of this was when he asked the headteacher of a school in our city if she would like a member of our church team, who listen to God, to come to the school to share God's word with her about the school. The teacher, who was not a Christian, agreed. An appointment was set up and Simon asked the Lord for a word of knowledge, to help this lady know God was speaking to her. Simon went to see her with the head of our children's ministry, and this is his account of what happened:

"I saw two visions. The first was of a white van pulling up outside the school. I saw the headteacher thrown out the back of the van and just left on the street standing alone with her bags. The second image I saw was her trying to dig a hole in sand, but the sides kept collapsing in and the hard work was undone. But then planks of wood began to be put in place and it stopped caving in. I shared these impressions and said that I felt God was saying that when she arrived at the school, she felt abandoned and just left with no help, and that she had also felt like no matter how hard she'd worked, things had just caved in. But now God had begun to add people to stand with her in the work and there had been a big shift.

The teacher responded and said, 'I mustn't cry, it's not professional, but that is a perfect description of what has been going on.'

At this point the Lord told me to tell her, 'The Lord is telling me that you can feel his presence if you'd like to' and I asked her if she would like that. She said 'yes'. I took her hand and said, 'Lord, let her feel your presence now.' The presence of God flooded the room and she began to cry and say, 'Wow!' We then had the privilege of leading her in a prayer of commitment to Jesus and she began her relationship with him."

Evangelist

The evangelist's role is giving the Good News of Jesus to others, bringing people to faith in God, and helping the Church to do this more effectively. They naturally spend time with people outside the church who aren't Christians – they enjoy doing this and naturally talk about their faith in these contexts. They are "people people" and others are drawn to them. They share their faith readily and can be bold in taking risks doing this. They are used by God to teach others how to do this and to move the church outwards.

If you have an evangelist in your missional community they will be the ones who are always inviting people to Alpha and sharing stories of how they shared their faith with people spontaneously. Their role is to help us grow in confidence. Naturally speaking we see the evangelistic personality in sales people, politicians, and public relations professionals. In the Bible we see examples like Philip explaining the

Christian faith to the Ethiopian official in his chariot.

When you are on mission you need to encourage others in the church to join you, because this is a key reason why God has gifted you in this way – to encourage others in mission. In your daily life you may well find conversations about faith happening naturally and you may well have a freedom to talk about Jesus with strangers. And you are able to ask the question that leads people to the decision to give their lives to Christ. You relate to Jesus on mission when he is building relationships with people outside of God's people and leading them to trust in him, as he did with Zacchaeus the tax collector.

But I have also seen many evangelists who need to mature in their gift and sharpen their practices. Think about where you get stuck in the process of making another disciple. Do you ever get past inviting people to Alpha? Do you know how to share Bible stories or deliver a clear explanation of the Gospel?

The challenge for evangelists is to actually make a disciple and not just a convert. Will you be willing to meet up regularly and disciple someone using Discovery Bible Study?

Pastor

The pastor cares for others. They have a tender and compassionate heart and are sensitive to the needs and feelings of others. They spend most of their time with other Christians within the life of the church, offering the support and care that they need. They have patience and time for other people. They are able to empathise easily and are often moved deeply by the pain of others. They are not focused on tasks and achievement and can find change difficult. The image from the Bible is one of a shepherd who cares for, guides, protects and provides for their flock. In church life they might fulfil this role through leading a cell group, a children's group, being part of the prayer for healing team, or simply within a small group be the person who is always looking out for people in need of support.

Counsellors, nurses, social workers or other caring professionals often have the pastoral personality and abilities. In the Bible we find Tabitha who was always doing good and caring for the poor (Acts 9:36) and Barnabas who God uses to encourage Paul and release him into ministry. He is known as *"the son of encouragement"* (Acts 4:36). When John-Mark let Barnabas and Paul down, and Paul was determined to press on without him (remember he was an apostle!), it was Barnabas who demonstrated his pastoral heart by choosing to stay with him and support him (Acts 15:36-40).

As a pastor you identify most with Jesus on mission when he stops to listen and share with someone, such as the disciples on the road to Emmaus (Luke 24). On mission you will naturally connect with people as you are warm and caring. And you will draw people closer to Jesus through you loving and supporting them. Keep doing this. You won't find street evangelism your natural environment, so don't worry about that, but maybe do it occasionally to challenge yourself. Long term friendships are more your cup of tea.

The issue for you will be whether you will risk your relationship with someone in order to bring the challenge of the Gospel. You will need to do this at times, so don't sell yourself short. Practice how to share your, and God's, story. But your loving others will draw them into the Christian community and the evangelists and apostles can help with the challenge then, after which you can continue to disciple them. You will find offering to pray with people and sharing life with them the most natural tools to use. As someone comes to faith you will naturally want to carry on the relationship and disciple them.

Cathi is a natural pastor. She is a mentor mother figure (dare I say, grandmother figure) to many in the church. But when she was having a coffee in town she felt prompted to talk to a young woman called Marta. Through this Cathi was able to pray with Marta and helped her childhood faith to come alive. Since then, Cathi has met with Marta regularly and mentored her and enabled Marta to come to faith, receive healing, and start serving God. Marta, on the other hand, is a natural evangelist and has led three people to faith in the last couple of months and even baptised two of them herself! She is so grateful for Cathi pastoring her and acknowledges that without her some of the chaos of her life may well have overwhelmed her.

Teacher
Teachers teach and explain God's word and the Christian faith to others. They are always thinking about aspects of faith and how to help others understand it. They enjoy studying and learning new things. When they teach, their gifts come through in the excitement they show about the material they are talking about and the clarity with which they communicate. They are people who study God's word and get excited about learning more about God and his ways.

In church life they might use this gift to teach children, young people or adults, they may preach in a Sunday service or lead a training course, or simply lead the time of looking at God's word in a cell group.

In general life we see this ability in teachers, lecturers and trainers. Paul had trained up a young man, Timothy, to lead a church and he wrote to him and said,

"The things you have heard me say in the presence of many witnesses entrust to reliable people who will also be qualified to teach others ... Do your best to present yourself to God as one approved, a worker who does not need to be ashamed and who correctly handles the word of truth." (2 Timothy 2:4,7,15)

This shows how important the teacher is, as they receive the truth of the Christian faith and are entrusted with passing it on to the next generation who will then teach others. It is vital that a church has people to do that in every area of its life, so that God's word is taught faithfully and people grow up in faith. When sharing faith, the teacher will naturally be able to explain things and find ways to help people understand things. You may enjoy apologetics and being able to knock down arguments set up against the Christian faith, persuading people of the rational basis for having faith in Jesus.

You identify most with Jesus on mission when he is teaching or debating with people, such as when he is answering Nicodemus' questions (John 3). But try and avoid entering into arguments. Practice using different tools, such as releasing God's presence through prayer and the gifts of the Spirit, so that you learn to let God lead you on mission. The danger is that you focus on truth and lack real connection with people. You may need to work on your relational skills and allow the Holy Spirit to develop compassion for people around you.

PRESS PLAY

Take some time to reflect on what area of ministry God has gifted you in. Sometimes it feels like there is a combination of two rather than one pure one. What does that help you to understand about your missional shape? How does this release you from wrong expectations? What challenges do you need to respond to? If you are struggling to decide which area is the best fit for you, try the survey online at: http://fivefoldsurvey.com. This is a tool you can work on with others, so if you are struggling to find your shape then ask others what they see in you. If you are confident in your main area of gifting then it can be helpful to find someone who is more experienced in that area to talk to about growing in that gifting. Equally, once you know your area then you can look to find others with other giftings, so they can support you in aspects of mission where you are weaker. This is why God has put you together with others on mission.

Personal or Group Study
IN

How are you?

Is there something you are thankful for?

If you were to choose which body part you are in the body of Christ, which one would it be and why?

UP John 21:1-22

Read John 21:1-22

What does this teach us about God?

(Reflect on what Jesus reveals about God and his relationship with us in the way he interacts with Peter)

What does this teach us about people?

(Think about the struggles Peter goes through in this passage to receive God's call and his insecurities, and what this says to you)
How do you need to respond?

OUT

Where are you serving at the moment?
Is this the right place?
Is there anything else you need to do to be confident in your general ministry area?
Who do you need to have a conversation with about this?
How can you work together with others on this?

5
Eating Together:
sharing our lives with others

Introduction

"Because we loved you so much, we were delighted to share with you not only the gospel of God but our lives as well." (1 Thessalonians 2:8)

It is fascinating how important meals are in the life of Jesus. Jesus had a great reputation for eating and drinking with the "wrong" kind of people – and the fact this angered the Pharisees so much shows something of the significance which people saw in sharing a meal together. The stories Jesus told to explain the kingdom often involved food – the celebration when the prodigal son returned, the banquets and wedding feasts. And, of course, most significantly we are given a meal to remember Jesus by. Through bread and wine we "commune" with him and the Spirit ministers his body and blood to us.

Jesus' meals were extraordinarily important. They were, in fact, pictures in miniature of what the kingdom of Heaven looks like. They were open and inclusive. Prostitutes, tax collectors and sinners came and wined and dined with Jesus, much to the irritation of the religious legalists. They believed in exclusion. He believed in embrace. Jesus therefore held banquets for the broken and feasts for the outcasts. Why? Because the kingdom of Heaven, as Stanley Hauerwas once said, "is the kind of meal where you find yourself sitting next to someone you normally wouldn't be seen dead with!" This is *Mission-Shaped Grace*.

Jesus' table is the kingdom. It's the place where Jesus says, "You can come as you are." It is also the place where he says, "No one is staying as they have been." Jesus held meals for messed up people because it's the kindness of God that leads to repentance, and then they repented, as Zacchaeus demonstrated. Jesus' meals were radical because they combined inclusion and transformation.

So what is it about eating together that is so profound? I think it is in the sharing of food together that a deeper bond is built between people. There is also the sense of being able to slow down and share ourselves with people as the coffee is sipped or the meal served. Our greatest need, other than salvation, is loving relationship. This is increasingly hard to find in the fragmented, selfish culture we live within. As Mother Theresa said:

"The greatest disease in the West today is not TB or leprosy, it is being unwanted, unloved, and uncared for. We can cure physical diseases with medicine, but the only cure for loneliness, despair, and hopelessness is love. There are many in the world who are dying for a piece of bread, but there are many more dying for a little love. The poverty in the West is a different kind of poverty – it is not only a poverty of loneliness, but also of spirituality. There's a hunger for love, as there is a hunger for God."

Eating together is a symbol of sharing our lives with others and including them in our communities. In a world where people are hungry for love and for God, there can be nothing more loving we can do for someone than to share a meal with them. So think about eating with others, but also think more widely about sharing your life with others.

Principle

As we have already seen, Jesus sent out the seventy-two to go into villages ahead of him (see Luke 10:1-11). He told them to find a home where a "person of peace" welcomed them. They were to stay in that home, eat their food and share the Good News, heal them and bring them freedom. So we have to look for "people of peace" and live with a sense of being "sent" to people in the same way that Jesus' disciples were. We need to be intentional in our desire to share our lives with others. As Alan Hirsch and Lance Ford say, "Sharing meals together on a regular basis is one of the most sacred practices we can engage in as believers. Missional hospitality is a tremendous opportunity to extend the kingdom of God. We can literally eat our way into the kingdom of God! If every Christian household regularly invited a stranger or a poor person into their home for a meal once a week, we would literally change the world by eating!"

So here are three things to think about from this passage as we share our lives with people of peace:

Time

The disciples were told to stay in a person's home if they were welcome and, in the context of sharing their lives with them, they were to heal the sick and proclaim the kingdom. This is a picture of us sharing our lives with people outside of the church and seeking to bless them. Are there people who you see regularly, share needs with, visit each other's homes, enjoy social time with? Each of us will probably eat 3 meals each day, so 21 meals every week. Who could you share one of those with? The beauty of thinking how to share our lives with others through a meal is that we are not adding another activity to our busy schedules, we are simply including them in what we are already doing – eating food and drinking coffee. So all you have to do is invite someone for a meal. Who could you invite in the coming week?

Team

Note that the disciples went in pairs and not alone. Eating together is not simply about us sharing food with people of peace, but with our Christian community as well. We need to be loving one another and encouraging one another in mission. We need people within the church to practice these principles, who will hold us accountable for sharing the Gospel with others, and who we can be a family with on mission together. Then, when we find our people of peace, we don't have to share our lives and eat with them on our own, we can do it with other Christians. Through our shared relationships they can begin to be part of our communities and discipleship can start even before they come to faith.

Task

Remember our task is to love our neighbour. But the most loving thing we can ever do for someone is to help them come to know God and receive his forgiveness and love. Within the context of sharing a home with these people of peace, the disciples were to tell them the Good News and release

God's presence into their homes. This only happened once the relationship had been established. When Jesus called the tax collector Matthew to follow him, as soon as Matthew had the chance he hosted a party at his home and invited all of his tax collecting friends to come and meet Jesus. This is the challenge for us as we invite and host and eat with others – to see how we can enable them to encounter Jesus. It is a context in which we can love, bless and share with friends using the other missional practices.

Presence

As we are present with people, Jesus is present with us. Through our friendship we are able to bless someone with Jesus' peace. This makes even the simplest time of eating or having a coffee with someone full of possibilities. An example of this is Alpha. With no disrespect to Nicky Gumbel, who has been such a gift to the Church in this country, the teaching is not the reason for the success of Alpha – it is the meal and the Alpha Away-Day. Eating together, building friendships and sharing lives are the key ingredients, in an environment in which people are full of the Holy Spirit.

Practice

The first challenge for us is whether we know anyone who is not a Christian well enough to invite them for a meal. If not, then we need to ask ourselves how we have become so disconnected from the wider community around us. We have to intentionally create opportunities to meet our neighbours, to get to know our work colleagues on a personal level, or join a club or community activity in order to find the people with whom God wants us to share his love. Once we have done this we look for opportunities to bless people and talk about faith. As we do this we need to share our lives with them. Too often we see evangelism in terms of finding someone to invite to a Christian event or Alpha. Invitational evangelism is great, but it is only authentic if we are genuinely loving and living alongside our friends. Eating together is a great way to maintain long term friendships because we all need to eat. Then within our Christian communities we can connect our friends with other Christians by sharing meals together and other social occasions. If we are sharing our lives with people, praying for them, and having conversations about faith, then we will know what will help them take steps closer to faith in Jesus. Then, when the time is right, our invitation to meet up to read a Bible passage together and talk about it, won't seem as if it comes out of the blue. One tool that can help is here is to use some different Bible passages known as the Seven Commands. Using the pattern of Discovery Bible Study the first two of the Seven Commands are great ways to introduce the need for your friend to decide to follow Jesus, then the others take them through some of the basic commands of Jesus.

7 Commands:

   i) Repent and believe (Luke 19:1-10)
   ii) Be baptised (Acts 8:26-40)
   iii) Pray (Matthew 6:5-15)
   iv) Make disciples (John 4:4-42)
   v) Love (Luke 19:25-37)
   vi) Celebrate the Lord's Supper (1 Corinthians 11:23-29)
   vii) Give (Mark 12:41-44)

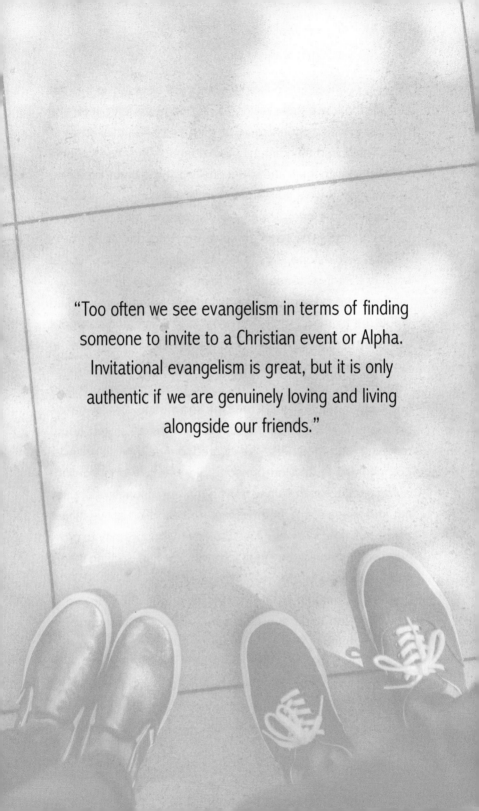

"Too often we see evangelism in terms of finding someone to invite to a Christian event or Alpha. Invitational evangelism is great, but it is only authentic if we are genuinely loving and living alongside our friends."

Sharing our lives is a principle of being a disciple, so it is not just for those we are seeking to see come to faith, it is also the way in which people grow as disciples when they come to faith. They need a community to belong to. They need people to meet up with them and intentionally disciple them, providing an example of what it means to live as a disciple.

Lorraine has been leading a discipleship group of some young women who have come to faith recently at St Paul's Church, Addlestone. This is how she describes the effect of sharing their lives together and being a "family on mission".

"From the beginning I was clear that nothing we studied would be in theory only. For example, if we studied about being in God's presence, then we spent time together in silence waiting on the Lord and studying the Bible. If we talked about praying for others, we spent time listening to each other, waiting for words of knowledge, laying hands on each other for healing and revelation. If we talked about reaching out to others, we shared our faith with friends, got involved in mission projects, did street or door-to-door outreach, and even helped start a monthly "songs of praise" tea and cakes event for local care homes." And as we talked about building community we took every opportunity to grow our own friendships by meeting up for a coffee, sharing meals and celebrating birthdays.

Another member of the group, Kati, reflects, "The group has given me hope that God can even use me and my life journey to help others. We started studying Acts, and started talking about how it would be great to go out and do some outreach on the streets. Going to New Wine and listening to all the speakers there was really inspiring. I felt God saying now is the time to step out in faith. When we got home our group went out to our local high street to talk to people about faith and the Alpha course coming up. Then a couple of us got involved with some door-to-door knocking on a new estate near the church. For me it is the learning together and praying that has given me the confidence to go out, and the Holy Spirit compelling us to try and spread the word."

PRESS PLAY

Who are you planning to eat with or share another activity with this week?

Who are you "on mission" with?

Do you have a person of peace who you are sharing your life with and praying for? If not, start praying and looking for who this is

Is it time to tell them God's story and invite them to read the Bible with you?

Individual / Group Study
IN

How are you?

What are you thankful for?

What has been your favourite time of sharing a meal with someone and why?

UP

Read Luke 10:1-11

What does this tell us about God?

(Think of Jesus in this passage and what he reveals about God)

What does this tell us about people?

(Think how the 72 felt and what Jesus asked them to do)

How do you need to respond?

OUT

Who will you invite for a meal or coffee?

Take time to pray for your people of peace. Make plans to meet up with them soon

What would be the next step of walking alongside them and sharing their lives as they move closer to faith in Jesus?

Don't Get Stuck

As you grow in these missional tools, don't see them as separate practices to tick off because they all work together. They are different tools in the toolkit of the apprentice disciples of Jesus that we are. We can choose when to pick up each tool as we allow Jesus to send us. Eating a meal and sharing conversation are vital partners, as is the desire to bless our person of peace, and a willingness to release God's presence into their lives, or meet up to read the Bible with them. And so we begin to see how these work together to enable us to live the life Jesus is calling us to.

You can identify some steps in the disciple-making process which these tools connect with. This is helpful so that you can see where you are in this process and where you might be "stuck", and which skills you still need to develop.

If you ever played "stuck in the mud" as a child you'll know that a key aspect of the game is getting "unstuck" by someone. Without that you cannot start to move again. In my conversations with Christians about mission I have found it helpful to ask them, "Where are you stuck?" Ask yourself the same question and it will help you to identify the next step to take and identify what issue you need to overcome.

It will also stop you becoming overwhelmed by trying to start each of these practices all at the same time. If you do, you'll probably have a really good try, fail and never try again. The process of discipleship is simply a long walk of obedience in the same direction, being willing to keep taking the next step. So the key question is, "What is your next step?"

The other reason that "stuck in the mud" is a good illustration is because we need one another to keep us going on this life of making disciples. Having someone else to challenge, support and hold us accountable for doing what we have said we are called to do is one of the reasons God has put us in the church together. As has been said, "the plural of disciple is church" – it is when our relationships as Christians become shaped by mission that the Church becomes the missionary disciple-making movement we are called to be.

Someone I talked to recently was frustrated because she'd had many conversations about faith and had shared her story and prayed with people, but no one had come to faith. "Why doesn't it ever go any further than this?" she asked. I could then explain that she had got stuck at the stage where she never took the opportunity to ask any of those people if they would like to meet up to talk more, or to look at some stories of Jesus.

The key aspect of "stuck in the mud" is that you need someone else to "unstick" you. The mutual support and accountability of another Christian or Christians is vital in growing in these tools and sustaining a missional lifestyle. Find others who you can read and discuss the Bible stories with, pray for "people of peace" together or practice the tools and pray for each other. And make sure you ask each other the challenging questions.

Annette is someone who really does seek to live as a missional disciple. She shares her faith with colleagues and friends, offers to pray with people and invites friends to connect with our church community. While she would say that she is far from the finished article, I asked her what enabled her to keep going in mission and she said very clearly, "My prayer triplet." Annette prays with her two prayer partners about mission and they encourage one another to keep going.

Below is a way of examining these practices as a process of making another disciple, with some associated questions to help you to know where you might be stuck. They are presented as "stepping stones" because it is often because we have failed to move from one stage to another that we are stuck. These are the '6C's' of disciple-making and every step is vital.

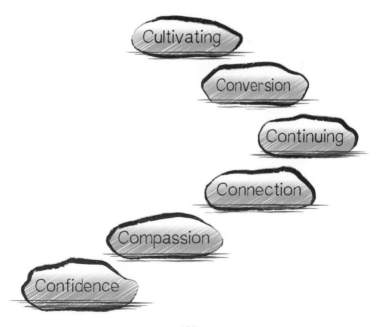

1. Confidence: filled with the Spirit and confident in the Gospel

Our daily reading of Scripture, prayer, and asking the Spirit to fill us, are fuel for the fire of mission. Regularly asking people to pray for us and lay hands on us for the filling of the Spirit keeps our faith alive and gives us a testimony of his work in our lives. Reading God's word means that we have his word in our hearts and we know the power of it in our lives. It is then that we have something to release and share with others and God is able to lead and guide us. It is in the power of the Spirit that we are sent on mission.

Are you confident in the Gospel and filled with the Spirit? Is there an overflow of God from your life? Do you need to seek God's renewing touch through his word and Spirit?

2. Compassion for the lost

Compassion for people characterised Jesus' life and it will ensure that our motivation in mission comes out of love. Out of our love for our friends and family who do not know Jesus we commit to pray for them each day for their salvation.

Have you mapped your relational world?

Are you praying daily for people to come to faith?

Are you living with a concern and compassion for the spiritual state of your friends and family?

Do you need to come back to the cross and remember all that Jesus did to save people, and what it tells us about the seriousness of living without God's love and forgiveness?

Ask God to show you his love and give you his compassion for your friends and family.

3. Connect

Sharing your lives with people you're praying for is the start of this stage: inviting people for a meal, sharing common interests, building relationships at the school gate, taking time to get to know a colleague, stopping to chat to a neighbour. All of those people will be in different places spiritually. Discovering who God has prepared to hear the Gospel is the next job and it is really a fishing expedition. As those called to fish for people we need to learn to use our nets – the missional practices we have been looking at.

Have you learned to tell your story?

Have you practiced praying for others for blessing and healing?

Are you seeking to listen to God for others?

If you answer "no" to any of the above questions then you are not really intending to do any of those things with people. So maybe the place you are stuck is in the learning and practicing of these skills.

Or maybe it is the actual doing it that is the issue? So here is your challenge:

Who in your life has a need that you could offer to pray with them about?

Who will you share your story with in the next week?

4. Continue: Stay with them: serve, share, be served

This is the stage that often lasts the longest as we walk with our friends through the ups and downs of their lives. Once we have shared and seen someone welcome prayer or indicate their openness to the Gospel, we have to decide what to do next to lead them closer to Jesus and when to offer it.

Is it an invitation to meet up and look at some stories from

Jesus' life and talk about faith? (if so, meet regularly and use Discovery Bible Study tools)

Is it offering to explain why you follow Jesus and sharing the Three Circles Presentation with them?

Is it an invitation to Alpha or involvement in a missional community?

Is it blessing them and serving them or letting them serve you?

Maybe you could offer them a book to read or YouTube clip to watch?

Ultimately, at this stage of the process you are looking to start to meet up consistently to share Gospel stories and explain who Jesus is. But this stage can take a long time; on average from the first contact with a Christian it can take a woman three years to come to faith and a man five years. So keep praying and loving and sharing.

5. Conversion: Lead them to faith in Jesus and be baptised

As you continue with your person of peace you are looking for moments where they have obviously started to follow Jesus and they need to know they have made this decision. Or they need help to get from a generally positive experience and attitude towards the Christian faith, to a clear response to Jesus. Everyone's journey is different but we need to be able to bring moments of challenge to follow Jesus and to see how they respond. The Three Circles presentation is one tool to test where they are and where they want to be. The first two of the 7 Commands Gospel stories will also do this. The other clear moment of challenge is whether they are ready to be baptised.

The Church has lost an understanding of the importance

of baptism. It is a clear command of Jesus in the Great Commission and so the process of leading someone to put their faith in Jesus must involve an explanation of and an encouragement to be baptised. The challenge to be baptised brings people to a clarity about their relationship with Jesus, and when they are baptised God applies the freedom and grace of his Spirit to their lives. We need to be willing to bring people to a point of decision to follow Jesus.

6. Cultivate: Disciple them and teach them to make disciples

Including people within our Christian community can happen at any point in the process, but at this stage it is vital. Equally, as we continue to meet one-to-one with the new disciple we must make sure that they start to learn the missional practices that will help *them* make a disciple. We must not wait until new disciples have been Christians for many years before teaching them how to make another disciple. The greatest opportunity they have is as Jesus transforms their life and their existing friends and family notice. Then they can tell their story.

Jesus spoke, healed and ministered differently to everyone he met. Each person's needs were different, so he loved and served them according to their need. Every person God brings to us to disciple will be different, so we need to use each of the tools we have learned differently. We allow the Holy Spirit to lead us, give us courage and wisdom, innovate and lead people to faith in Jesus.

I encourage you to have people to share the journey with, like running mates. Together you can encourage one another, hold each other accountable for the things you have said you will do, and when one is struggling others can support them.

The other reason for sharing these principles with other Christians is that you can practice them together. Each *Grace Notes* tool has a practice section and is deliberately named because you will need to practice them. Reading these chapters alone will not bring about lasting change in your life as a disciple, and using the tools once will not bring you to that place where you can do them without thinking about it.

There is the old joke about the tourist in New York City who asks "How do I get to Carnegie Hall?" (a famous concert hall), and is given the answer, "Practice, practice, practice!"

When you share these *Grace Notes* with others you have the chance to practice them together.

In New York every year they hold a ticker tape parade celebrating the Fire Service. The parade includes all of the fire service personnel with engines and bands and baton twirlers. Behind all of this are the people who have been rescued by the Fire Service throughout the year. They follow the parade and the crowds celebrate the lives that have been saved. When I arrive in God's presence at the end of my life, surrounded by the great cloud of witnesses, I want to be able to look behind me and see the people I will share eternity with because I shared the Good News of Jesus Christ with them.

Hollywood loves stories that involve rescuing people from extreme situations – whether it is *Appollo 13*, *Saving Private Ryan* or *The Martian*. Enormous resources are used and great risks taken, to rescue one person. God is calling you to offer the resources of your life in partnership with the resources of the Gospel and his Spirit to rescue people of infinite value to him. Will you do it? Will you be a missional disciple? Will you allow the grace of God to flow through you to others by living a mission-shaped life? You were made for it. There is no better way to live than the adventure of being on mission with Jesus.

And so we finish with a blessing for those willing to step out of their comfort zones and onto the path of following in the footsteps of Jesus:

Traditional Gaelic Blessing

May the road rise up to meet you
May the wind always be at your back
May the sun shine warm upon your face
and rains fall soft upon your fields
And until we meet again
May God hold you in the palm of His hand

"We have a lot to unlearn —
centuries of practices and
assumptions that fundamentally
undermine the mission-shaped
church Jesus always intended us to
be. You will need courage to start
this journey..."

Epilogue:
A note to church Leaders

This book is about personal missional practices. But there are
no individual Christians in the New Testament and the Church
is the *ekklesia* of God – the gathered and sent people of God.
As leaders it is our responsibility to create communities that
make disciples who will make disciples. C.S. Lewis describes
it this way:

"The Church exists for nothing else but to draw people into
Christ, to make them little Christs. If they are not doing that,
all the cathedrals, clergy, missions, sermons, even the Bible
itself, are simply a waste of time. God became human for
no other purpose. It is even doubtful, you know, whether the
whole universe was created for any other purpose. It says in
the Bible that the whole universe was made for Christ and
that everything is to be gathered together in Him."

This may seem clear, but the Church in the West faces
two massive challenges. First, it has been shaped on the
basis of an attractional/pastoral model of mission. The parish
system created a church building and a vicar for every local
community and the model of mission was of the local minister
pastorally caring for those in their parish. Anyone outside of

the regular Sunday worshipping community is invited to join with many points of entry on offer. So the Church lost sight of its call to equip people to go and represent Christ and share the Gospel.

But the second challenge is that our society has increasingly rejected the Christian faith and people no longer understand the basics of the Gospel or think about attending church as they did in the past. Trying to attract people to events in church buildings does not work anymore, however great your band is and however tasty your doughnuts are. This has left the Church wedded to a redundant model and marooned in the midst of a sea in which people around us are lost, but we have forgotten how to reach and rescue them. The things we have been doing don't work anymore and the evidence of declining numbers, especially among younger generations, is stark.

The solution is to equip people to be missional disciples. But to do this we need to see big shifts in the practices and culture of our church communities. Dave Ferguson of Exponential fame summarises what needs to happen in the following equation:

Missional Church + Missional People = Missional Movement

This shows that our churches need to start to be defined and shaped by mission. No longer can we focus on a church's seating capacity, as if the aim is to get more people to attend a Sunday service in a church building. Instead, we must focus on a church's sending capacity – how effective it is at sending people out on mission. This will mean establishing a culture in which the vision and values of a church are clearly focused on reaching lost people. Then we need the vehicles that will take us to that destination, reshaping our Sunday gatherings and establishing ways in which people can go out on mission together and grow as disciples.

Then we need to equip them in missional practices. It is not enough to exhort people to be evangelistic without training them. Exhortation without training creates guilt.

What will this mission-shaped church look like? Below is a comparison of some of the differences between the pastoral church and the missional church:

Pastoral Church	Missional Church
Congregational focus	Focus on kingdom expansion
Sunday is the destination	Sunday is launching place
Fellowship groups	Missional communities
Passive membership	Active membership
Aim is to retain members	Aim is to release members
No spiritual warfare	Wins spiritual battles
Leaders = rule keepers	Leaders = risk takers
People to fulfil programme	Programme equips people
Neat and tidy	Messy
Finances for maintenance	Finances for mission

So we have a lot to unlearn – centuries of practices and assumptions that fundamentally undermine the mission-shaped church Jesus always intended us to be. You will need courage to start this journey. There is no guarantee of success, and in the short term it can feel painful as we seek to help people understand that the way we have taught them to live out their faith is not the true picture of discipleship we find in Scripture.

But as leaders of God's people we are the ones he has

chosen to navigate this new territory. Discipleship is not about results, it is about obeying our Master, and he who calls us is faithful. You have the privilege and opportunity to lead the people entrusted to you out of these restrictions and to begin to see them become the missionary people of God that they are.

At the time of writing, Holy Trinity Church Leicester has been following a missional communities strategy for seven years. Much of what I have written is borne out of the generosity and faith of fantastic people who have been willing to have a go and take some risks, make some mistakes and keep going. I thank God for them every day. It has been tough and frustrating, but it is full of hope and joy as we go on this adventure following Jesus. We feel incompetent and we have so much to learn, and we are not even sure what it is meant to look like in the end. But I really do believe God is doing a new "old" thing among his Church and awakening us to who we were always called to be. Aslan is on the move, the winter is over and the new shoots of Spring are coming through the ground.

When the Israelites were about to cross into the Promised Land, God spoke to Joshua and said,

"'When you see the ark of the covenant and the Levitical priests carrying it, you are to move out from your positions and follow it. Then you will know which way to go because you have never been this way before...' And Joshua told the people, 'Consecrate yourselves, for tomorrow the Lord will do amazing things among you.'" (Joshua 3:3-5)

Great words to leave us with. How will we lead the church forward into unknown territory? Trust in God's power and presence, allow the Holy Spirit to lead us, and live with hope for the great things God will do as we step forward. Let's consecrate ourselves to God.

Bibliography:

A Passionate Life, Mike Breen, Walt Kallestad, Kingsway, 2005.

Mere Christianity, C.S. Lewis, Collins, 1952.

Movements That Changed the World, Steve Addison, IVP USA, 2011.

What Jesus Started, Steve Addison, IVP USA, 2013.

The Great Omission, Dallas Willard, Monarch Books, 2006.

The Spirit of the Disciplines, Dallas Willard, Harper San Francisco, 1991.

Life With God, Richard Foster, Hodder & Stoughton, 2009.

Leadership Jazz, Max DePree, Doubleday, 1992.

The Cost of Discipleship, Dietrich Bonhoeffer, Prentice Hall & IBD, 1963.

Right Here Right Now, Alan Hirsch and Lance Ford, Baker Books, 2011.

Making Disciples: How Did Jesus Do It? Tony Pullin, CWR, 2014.